WHO SAYS YOU
CAN'T?

Timeless Lessons and Experiences in Business

FRANK NNEJI

Founder, ABC Transport Plc

Frank Nneji is the founder of ABC Transport Plc, a road transportation and logistics company with a fleet of over 500 vehicles, more than 1,500 employees and offices in 32 locations including Accra, Togo and Benin Republic.

Nneji has been credited with revolutionizing Nigeria's road transportation industry with innovative ideas and entrepreneurial initiatives that have influenced practices and policies in very significant ways. He holds degrees from the University of Nigeria, Nsukka (UNN), the Lagos Business School and Wharton Business School, USA. He is an Officer of the Order of the Niger (OON).

" I am always thinking of how to do things better and add value. When you achieve this, good things often follow. This is my most important concept in business. The desire to add value to society, to take risks and create wealth while doing so, have motivated me for many years. "

Frank Nneji, 2018

Produced in Nigeria

Published by Storyteller Services

Lagos, Nigeria.

ISBN NO: 978-978-965-139-9

For enquiries:

+234 816 836 0168 or +234 803 960 0958

Designs by Visualview

Dedication

To my lovely wife Ngozi, for her support, understanding and patience, especially during the formative years of my business ventures.

To that first set of ABC drivers – Peter, Lucky, Isaac, Felix, Christopher and Hyacinth – who, despite the doubts about the prospects of a new 'style' in the road transport industry in Nigeria, stuck with me to establish ABC Transport. Their faith in the dream was inspiring.

CONTENTS

Foreword

I often begin my entrepreneurship classes by reminding participants that venturing is an imperative of being, citing, for people of faith, Genesis 2:15 in which man is invited to be a co-creator with God, moving creation down the path of its full promise.

Sadly, most men and women fail to respond to this duty of creation for a variety of reasons, including the fear of failure, lack of knowledge and self-doubt. But from the testimonies of those who have dared to venture, they may find confidence, and be inspired.

Close to home in providing example is the story of Frank Nneji. It is one that I have been familiar with for most of the half century he has doggedly pursued entrepreneurial life.

Frank saw the light early, beginning in his undergraduate days at the University of Nigeria (UNN). It has been nearly twenty years since the first case study on Rapido Ventures, his presentation and classroom equipment enterprise, was chronicled under my supervision by one of my younger colleagues at the Lagos Business School. I continued to adapt that case as Frank identified a dissatisfaction gap in how people got around in Nigeria, when the airline business was a monopoly of the State and brought great grief to travelers. His decision to position ABC Transport as an alternative to air travel, rather than the well-established interstate bus lines with their orthodoxies, was ground breaking.

In this memoir, Frank Nneji sets out to challenge the young to the fact that they too can. I concur and say to the reader in the words of Nobel Laureate Wole Soyinka, "you need to set forth at dawn". That, indeed, was what Frank did, transiting from an entrepreneurial undergraduate to a 23 years old founder of a formal company.

Frank Nneji sets out very young and unveils a lifetime of challenges and the rewards of daring to believe in the prospects of creating venture.

What a joy it is for me to see this day and the chronicling of this journey. Entrepreneurs help solve social problems and derive economic and other benefits for being leaders and change agents. Central to their essence is passion and recognition that failure is an opportunity to learn lessons that will prevent more failure, so they fall and rise again. In this book, Frank provides twelve captivating chapters of storytelling and teachings from the experiences and wise words of others with the ultimate lesson: 'People Determine Everything'. So true. Watching him receive an award from ANAMMCO/Mercedes Benz many years ago, I could tell that he had bridged the Knowing-Doing gap regarding understanding of the fact that people determine everything. He walked forward holding hands with one of his 'captains', the drivers that shaped the mystic and differential advantage of ABC Transport. Quite a wholesome read.

Pat Utomi (Prof.)
Founder,
Center for Value Leadership (CVL)

Acknowledgements

It has taken a lot of effort by people around me to get me to document this memoir.

My good friends George Emeghara and Austine Onwubiko, in the past seven years, persuaded me to write my story for the benefit of the young struggling entrepreneur. I thank them immensely for this push.

Peter Uche-Umez, the former head of customer service at ABC Transport also contributed to the zeal in writing this book. It was not until I got in contact with Olakunle Kasumu that the real actualization of this book commenced. I am most grateful to all of them.

I also thank Ngozi Okoli, Nneoma Anosike and Dozie Iheanacho of ABC Transport who at different times reviewed and processed imputes in this book.

Special appreciation goes to Sesan Oyebode of Novitas for preserving many of the past archived materials on ABC Transport, especially the adverts.

I feel that the story of my business life is still not half told, as I keep remembering many spectacular incidents in my start up story.

I thank God for His grace in all these.

Introduction

In 1983, I was twenty three years old when I started my first registered business, Rapido Ventures. I had just graduated from the University of Nigeria, Nsukka (UNN). Some argue that as a young person, it is better to start out working for an employer before venturing out to start a business. Though they have a point and I understand that perspective, I think it is, like the Americans will say, "different strokes for different folks" and what one chooses to do should depend on where one is going.

However, before I started Rapido Ventures, I did have a few minor job experiences. When I left secondary school in 1976 at age sixteen, I enlisted as an auxiliary teacher. That was during the time of Universal Primary Education (UPE) in Nigeria. At that time, there was an explosion in the number of primary school intakes and because there was a massive shortage of qualified teachers, the then military government of Olusegun Obasanjo deployed graduates from different fields to teach in schools across the country. They called them auxilliary teachers. My teaching job was for elementary four in a primary school not far from my village. I did that job from 1977 to 1978 before I got admitted into the University of Nigeria. I should point out that while at it, I was also selling clothes. I would get them from those who travelled out of the country and returned with options for sale. I would market the clothes to potential buyers and eventually have them sold, earning myself good money. I also used to go to Aba for fabrics to sell.

Another pre-Rapido Ventures job experience I had was during my National Youth Service Corps (NYSC) programme when I worked in an estate surveying firm for close to a year. The firm was into evaluation of the fish stock in oil- polluted areas of Rivers State, South-South of Nigeria.

And as for business experiences before I started Rapido Ventures, you will discover from subsequent pages in this book that right from my childhood, I amassed bits and pieces of education in commerce from buying and selling things and making money through services I provided to people. So, when I set out on my entrepreneurial journey after graduating, I had those little experiences that had given me a sense of confidence in my ability to crack things in business.

It is noteworthy to mention that I studied biological science at UNN and that was because my mother, who was a nurse, wanted me to become a medical doctor. As far as she was concerned, everyone had to get into the medical profession. It is perhaps the reason why my younger sister is a doctor; my brother, who runs ABC Transport with me, is a pharmacist by training and my two elder sisters are nurses. So biological science was for me, a preliminary course for medicine. Fortunately, after one year, I discovered I was not cut out for medicine. I tried to change to a business related course but when I found out that I was going to lose one year for that, I decided to just go ahead with biological science and learn business outside of school.

It was quite strange to Nigerians to see a 23-year-old graduate like me start a business at the time I did, rather than look for a nice office job. It was not unusual for me to hear someone say, "Hey, why don't you go and get a job to gain experience? Why are you wasting your life?" I remember the day I rented my 760 naira office and was trying to get my reading table which I had picked up from home, into the new office space as my working table. Two people stopped by that day and one who was an engineer asked, "What are you trying to do?" When I told him I was trying to get the table into my office, he said, "You young boys! Why don't you go and get a job to gain experience first? You are becoming too ambitious!" The second person stopped, looked at me while I was trying to get the table into my office and said in a most sarcastic way, "I wish you all the best" and walked away.

Since I had studied biological sciences at UNN and was familiar with laboratory equipment, I felt I could go into the area of supplying schools with laboratory and scientific tools and materials, so that became my first focus in my new business. I prepared catalogues by making photocopies of products in the catalogues of my suppliers, cut the pictures in those catalogues, pasted them on a blank piece of paper and made copies of them. It was not exactly the most innovative way to promote Rapido Ventures, but it sufficed, I have to say. My main customers at that time were the universities in the eastern part of Nigeria, particularly the Federal University of Technology, Owerri (FUTO). A few months after the inception of Rapido Ventures, I started thinking of going into a more specialized area. My thinking along that line was encouraged when FUTO ordered chalk boards from me and I went around looking for a supplier of good quality chalk boards in the country. Because it was tough finding one, I decided to start making them using particle boards which were treated with chemicals to produce a good writing surface. My house served as my first factory.

Early in 1984, I realized that many of my customers needed overhead projectors, so I thought I could start supplying them. After extensive research, I settled for a brand called 'Elite'. The Nigerian market for overhead projectors at that time was dominated by 3M products which were marketed by a UAC subsidiary company. However, the bulbs of the Elite Projectors were sold at N69 while the 3M Projector Bulbs sold at N350, giving the Elite Projectors a significant market edge. I pushed this advantage aggressively and eventually the Elite Projectors became more widely used. In mid-1984, I got Rapido Ventures to sign contracts with Elite and Magi Board of the United Kingdom for the sole distributorship of their products in Nigeria. Three years later, due to rising demands in Lagos, a branch of Rapido Ventures was opened there and another one was opened in Kaduna a year later.

I should also mention that I never prepared a business plan for Rapido Ventures. I just came up with the idea and moved on it. Don't get me wrong, I am not saying business plans are unnecessary because they are, but business, as in life generally, can't really be pigeonholed. One of the things I realized early is that if you have an appetite for learning, your experiences will always teach you a lot.

As I kept trying to develop Rapido Ventures during those early years, I observed that most companies who supplied presentation equipment only sold individual products and did not relate them to the presentation needs of the customers. The customers were usually not knowledgeable enough to decide what they required to solve their presentation needs. Consequently, the emphasis of Rapido Ventures was not just on selling individual products but also helping customers realize what they needed and offering solutions to those needs. I therefore focused on providing customers with handbooks on the use of presentation equipment and organized exhibitions for them.

Rapido's growth was phenomenal. Between 1984 and 1992, it was undoubtedly the major supplier of educational materials in Nigeria and indeed across West Africa. Between 1990 and 1996, the company's turnover had risen from N3.5m to N47.9m. By 1992, we had built a N4m factory at Owerri to produce flipcharts, magnetic boards, pin boards and projector stands. By 1997 our staff strength had grown to 81 and each salesman had a vehicle plus 3-5% commission on sales.

But it was not all rosy. At a point in time, growth in demand for audio visual training and presentation equipment started to slow down due to the crisis at the universities and difficulties in accessing funds. We responded to this by going into cassette duplicators, public address systems and computer imaging systems. I use Rapido Venture's story in this book mainly as a background to the story of Associated Bus Company (ABC), the road transport business I started a few years after pioneering Rapido and which today, has become a publicly quoted company and is one of the most respected brands in West Africa's business community. ABC Transport's tale is based on what you might refer to as my underlying business philosophy: to always seek ways to add value. People tend to be too focused on making money in business. I don't think that's the right attitude. I believe that when you add value, you make money. Consequently, I am always thinking of how to do things better and add value. When you achieve this, good things often follow. This is my most important concept in business. The desire to add value to society, to take risks and create wealth while doing so, have motivated me for many years.

ABC Transport for me, was all about the urge to run a transportation company that would guarantee dignity and comfort for the traveler. Long distance bus travels within Nigeria, prior to ABC Transport, were uncomfortable for travelers so when I started thinking seriously about the business, I thought it would be important to move from merely selling seats to selling comfort and decency. It was all about defining a niche. If ABC Transport was going to be in competition at all, it would be in competition with the airlines.

Today, I am proud of how that idea has grown into becoming a notable international brand that has expanded into the logistics, courier and hospitality sectors while employing thousands of people. Whenever I think about how the ABC Transport idea has germinated, I am astounded by the power we all have been endowed with to dream and realize our dreams; to start small and grow big; to become better and relevant and to positively influence the lives of others in amazing ways.

It is my privilege to share, in this book, some of my personal experiences in business and those lessons that have been crucial in giving me the little successes I have had. It will give me tremendous joy if my shared ideas and experiences inspire you to be the best you can be.

PART I

GETTING STARTED

CHAPTER ONE

A Glimpse into the Future
"It's the curious that innovates"

There are often particular experiences in everyone's past that are like indicators - or if you prefer, prophecies - one can, with the benefit of hindsight, refer to as significant previews to the future. One of mine was when I was five years old, living with my parents in our small, modest house in a village called Lagwa Okwuato which is about 3.5 kilometers away from my home town Ezuhu Nguru, in Aboh Mbaise Local Government, Imo State, South East of Nigeria. Mbaise is an amalgam of indigenous clans situated in the heartland of Igboland. Before European adventurers arrived in Mbaise, subsistence agriculture was the main source of living for people there and legend has it that the weekly gathering of male family members around the fresh palm wine keg constituted the forum for discussing important matters and taking major communal decisions.

But Lagwa Okwuato was home for us at that time not Mbaise. It was the kind of home where, even though modest, we were happy and contented. In many ways, it was your average home with its own dramas that would later form memories for the children and define their futures.

The Missing Clock

I was only about five years old when one day, someone realized that the small table clock we had in the house had gone missing. Everyone was bewildered by its disappearance. The older members of my family were mystified but not me because I was the one who had taken the clock when no one was watching. As the older ones searched, they didn't bother to ask me where the clock was, after all, what in the world would a five-year-old want to do with it? But I had taken the clock, walked to the back of the house, dug a hole and planted it with an innocent expectation that it would one day germinate and produce more clocks if I watered it regularly.

After some days, my siblings noticed I kept going behind the house to pour water on the same spot. I had obviously planted something there. They decided to dig whatever it was up and to their utmost shock, they found the missing table clock! It had become rusty and spoilt which was no surprise. My parents could only laugh at my childish stupidity.

Curiosity was what drove me to bury that clock to see if it could grow like seeds and plants I had observed. Curiosity was one of my stand out traits as a child and in many ways, it provided a glimpse into my future as an entrepreneur. I always wanted to know how things worked. I probed, I asked questions, I wondered. Many decades after the missing clock experience, it was curiosity that led me to start businesses and create solutions and value in the market place.

Swallowing the Coins

Another one of such childhood experiences happened one day when my mother was working as a midwife. Back then we used to hang around her a lot as she attended to patients. We would be by her side when men were ready to pay her after their wives had delivered. Mum would give them a bill of ten shillings for example but some couldn't afford such fees. They would either appeal to her to reduce the fee or allow them to pay in installments. There was an instance when she said to one of the men who pleaded with her to give him more time to pay up. "You have eaten my money, abi?" she said. It was a way of saying that the man had spent the money he was expected to pay her. The man spent the next hour pleading with my mother to spare him. When he left, I looked at her and asked with all the innocence of a child, "Do people eat money?" Probably in no mood to explain things or because she took my question lightly, she said, "yes" and turned back to focus on what she had been doing. But that response was serious enough for me. Some hours later, mum asked me about some coins she had kept with me. I told her I had eaten them and I was not joking at all. I had indeed swallowed the coins. She went nuts. Everyone started to panic. Things happened quickly. Someone put something in my anus, pumped in water and gave me a prescription that helped to excrete the coins. Needless to say that coins were kept away from me for a long time after that incident.

"Children, Be Curious" **– Jonathan Swift**

Another experience I had as a child was when an education

ministry inspector visited my primary school just before I was admitted as a pupil. It was then known as Christ the King School, a small institution in a village with no electricity supply. We had to use lanterns and lamps whenever it became dark in the evenings. After some time, my dad was able to buy a generator that helped to make life a lot better after 6pm.

Christ the King School was across the road from home. Back then, there were no nursery schools and only children who were six years old and above were admitted into primary schools. Before I became qualified I would spend my time on the school's field chasing butterflies, other insects and small animals that fascinated me. I had no cares in the world.

That particular day, the education ministry inspector arrived in an old model Fiat that marked him out as one of the elites in the village. He parked it and for whatever reason, perhaps because the car had a weak battery, left the engine running when he walked into the administrative building in the school. I stood there fascinated by the car yet alarmed by the smoke coming out of its exhaust pipe. I would not have been worried at all if I was used to cars but I didn't see them too often. When the inspector returned, the little me ran to him and asked, "Do you have fire under your car?" The surprised man said, "Why do you ask?" And I said, "Because there is smoke coming out of it." The man burst out into laughter and asked the headmaster, "Who is this child?" The headmaster responded, "His siblings attend this school. He is not old enough to join us yet, but it looks like he is already eager to do just that." "Who are his parents?" asked the impressed inspector. When he was told that our house was just across the road, he walked home with me to meet the parents of one of the most curious boys he had ever met.

That was me as a child and it's still me today. I have always asked, "Why is this so? Why can't we do things better? Why can't we try a different method? Why is this thing done this way and not that way?" My employees and colleagues know me for this. I keep on probing to challenge them to think out of the box.

I never stopped being curious and explorative as a child. When I was seven years old, the Nigerian Civil War started and the memory I have is that of an environment of refugees, malnourished children coming to feeding centers and my mother's maternity home serving as one of the designated centers for relief materials. It was actually 'Feeding Centers' they used to call it and the Red Cross workers would go there to prepare food and use the center to cater for kwashiorkor-stricken children.

Even at that young age, I wanted to join the Biafran Army. There was something called 'Boy's Company' where a young boy would be dressed in a uniform and made to serve one of the soldiers. I was involved in that. Almost every Igbo felt a sense of patriotism during Biafra. Everyone wanted to contribute and serve. Age didn't matter much. People felt they could offer something, no matter how little. By the time the war ended I was already ten years old and had missed a lot of schooling. The war had interrupted our formal education for at least one year because the regular school structures were easy targets for fighter jet pilots who simply dropped bombs on structures they felt could be camp grounds for Biafran soldiers. When we did resume school, there was something we called, 'Win the War School' which was a kind of make shift arrangement where you didn't necessarily have to be in any classroom to take lessons. You could go to a bush or under a tree to have classes. Such places were much safer than the more vulnerable school structures.

Just after the war, I met a gentleman popularly known then as, Mighty Joe. He was a young, enterprising trader who sold different commodities. My interest in Mighty Joe was to get a small loan from him. But what did a ten-year-old need a loan for? During and after the war, I had observed children hawking matches around for sale. What they did was to buy packs of matches, open them, and tie the match sticks in fives for sale. When I did my calculations, I thought it was a smart idea. So I went to Mighty Joe for a loan to get into the match stick selling business. I don't remember how much I asked for, maybe five pence or something close to that but whatever the amount was, Mighty Joe laughed hard at me. "Have you told your dad this?" he asked, trying to stifle his laughter. "No" I responded. "Go and tell your dad and If he asks you to go ahead with your plan, then you can come back for the loan". Of course, that was the end of my business plan because I didn't have the guts to go and tell my dad.

My First Transportation Service

Another significant experience I had was also after the Civil War, during my secondary school days. I noticed that students were keen on going to watch football matches and attending inter school events like debate competitions. "What if I can make transportation to those events easy for students?" I thought. It used to cost two to three pence for rides to many of those venues. My curiosity got me thinking about how I could explore the opportunity. I eventually came up with the idea of linking up with drivers of Mammy Wagons (that was the name given to the big lorries used to transport goods and people back in those days). The idea was to arrange with them to pick up students on particular days, at specified locations and fees. On the other hand, I would persuade students keen on being transported to the event venues to write down their names and pay some money for the trip. Once I had their money with me, I would simply pay the drivers their fees and pocket my own cut. If the lorry driver was expecting, say, two pounds, I would charge the students a little extra for myself and ensure the driver got the money he charged. It was pretty much a straightforward business and it earned me popularity in school.

It was the famous British author, Graham Swift who wrote:

> "Children, be curious. Nothing is worse than when
> curiosity stops. Nothing is more repressive than the

repression of curiosity. Curiosity begets love. It weds us to the world. It's part of our perverse, madcap love for this impossible planet we inhabit. People die when curiosity goes."

I believe curiosity births innovation and innovation is what sets entrepreneurs apart. The good thing is that curiosity is a trait we all come into this world with. Every child wonders. Every child asks, "Why?" It's just that many of us tend to lose this sense of wanting to dig deeper as we grow up. I'm glad that somehow, I never lost mine and it was while being curious, while asking questions and wondering why, that I stumbled upon the idea to build a road transport company that changed my life and my country.

Be Curious.

Always ask questions.

Never be satisfied
with the status quo.

Probe.

And then,
probe again.

Questions are what
give you answers.

My parents, siblings and I (2nd from left). It was a modest family yet my parents gave us lots of good memories.

My siblings and I (middle), about 1965

With my elder sister, about 1966

Like others, as a young child I was very curious. I asked questions a lot and sought solutions to everything I saw as a problem. Children are generally like this and it's a trait entrepreneurs need to successfully create values for society. The problem is that parents and society often suppress that curious trait in us before we hit our adolescent years. Never allow that curiosity in you to die. It's the basis for innovation and innovation is what drives business and our world in general.

CHAPTER TWO

The Question that Never Goes Away

*"Are you born an entrepreneur or are
you trained to become one?"*

I believe it is easy to tell if a young person can become a good entrepreneur. In the previous chapter, I narrated examples of experiences I had and traits I exhibited as a child that seemed to point to my future. Someone else might pass those stories as common for children and irrelevant, but I like to think that dots always connect in life. Burying a clock, watering and expecting it to grow and multiply as a five-year-old, was, as wildly speculative as it might sound, indicative of an entrepreneurial mindset because entrepreneurs are always looking at how to multiply resources, grow things, wait patiently and expect 'harvests'. They always want to conquer their environments and add value.

Some children's talents or callings are on display for the world to see but most times, adults around them take all the indicators for granted. Some other children have talents or abilities that adults mistake for misbehaviours or misdirected energy. If a child likes to arrange or sort out things in specific patterns or along colour lines, it may mean that he or she is an analytical thinker who pays attention to details. That may indicate an aptitude for science or mathematics. A parent who observes that needs to find ways of encouraging it. Some children tend more towards being around others while some other children prefer to be alone. Some are expressive, some are not. My point is that we can't take any trait for granted.

Business on Campus

By the time I got into the university, I had developed considerable aptitude for business. I had a flair for it. I was in biological sciences and students had to write a lot of lecture notes for the courses we were taking. There was Chemistry 111 and Biology 151 which had 12 credits. From the very first year, every student feared those courses. To pass them, students had to get past question papers and study them well enough to have an idea of how examiners structured

18

questions and how best to answer them.

I felt the situation presented a business opportunity for me. I thought that if I could compile the relevant past questions and made them into booklets for sale, I could exploit the ready-made market for such because students were desperate for anything that could help them pass those dreaded courses. So, I started packaging and selling past question papers. I would get the old question papers, take them to a typist to have them typed out, put the typed document in a stencil, cyclostyle and then bind.

I had a partner for the business. It was a guy from Nnewi called Nnodu Agu. Agu and I lived in Zik Flats, a compound with several flats that served as students hostel, located about four kilometers from the main campus of our university. Students always had to wait for a school bus to pick them up and take them to school. But Agu had a Yamaha model motorcycle and every morning, he would ride to school and get to the lecture room long before any other person arrived. He used to pick me up for those rides and that made us become friends. Therefore, when I needed a partner for the past questions business, it was a no brainer. Agu was my man. The past questions business thrived so much that from my second year in the university, it became unnecessary for me to ask my parents for money for school. By my third year, I was supporting my younger brother financially.

From the past questions business, I moved to trading clothes in school and Italy was the place to buy T-shirts, shoes, bags and other wears and accessories. The Nigerian Airways had special students rebates then. The ticket was N200 and they gave students a 50% cut. I started taking trips to Italy to get the best possible quality at the cheapest possible prices and return to Nigeria to sell them. I was not the only student in the business. I had a few other friends who got into it and at times two or three others would join us to travel to Italy, share rooms there, go to the market to buy the wears and return to school to sell them.

But going to Italy to buy the clothes and accessories was one thing, being able to sell them in school was another thing entirely and not everyone experienced the joy of selling the things they travelled all the way to Europe to buy. Some were forced to sell on credit but never got their money back. Some others ended up dumping what they sold in a store somewhere or giving them away because they simply couldn't get buyers.

Fortunately, I did not fall into that category and smart advertising may have had a lot to do with that. At the lobby of the hostel where I resided, was a mirror a lot of students used. You would always see my adverts on that mirror. I remember one that read, 'Buy Two Pairs For the Price of One'. That caught people's attention a lot and it attracted more buyers to my products. I had other creative advertising strategies I deployed and each one earned me popularity and sales.

There were students in my school who believed that the only thing they should ever do in school was read. There were others who only partied. And there were some who only engaged in religious activities. For me, school was about studying, doing business and creating some time to socialize.

Like I mentioned earlier, I studied biological science and when I was told I could change to business administration if I was ready to lose one year, I said, "No way!" I wanted to leave school as quickly as possible. So, I resolved to learn business on my own from real life experiences and studying. I used to always read Business Times which was published by Daily Times every week back then. It was a useful resource in terms of getting updates on the economy and business trends.

Transport Secretary

Another experience I had in school that is relevant and worth narrating, happened during my third year in the university when the position of transport director was introduced in the Students Union. Like I mentioned earlier, before then I had been involved in a small transport business moving students to venues of social and sports events, so I had developed interest in the whole idea of transportation. When the transportation director position became up for grabs, it caught my attention and I started thinking about running for the position. It seemed like an exciting idea to me and my curious nature only fueled a growing keenness. I was intrigued with the idea of being involved in student unionism and managing transportation for union leaders on campus. There was only one problem: Student Union activities were usually left to non-science students back then. That was the campus culture. There was a general notion that, in an academic sense, it was suicidal for science students to get deeply involved in student unionism. Getting involved, for science students, was deemed as resolving to fail.

But I was absolutely sold to the idea. I believed I could handle the job well. I developed a full manifesto and went all the way for it. It was a no contest eventually. I became the transport director for UNN. It turned out to be an incredible experience for me. I became very popular and left the position with a solid reputation as a high performer in the Students Union Government. I remember a headline in the campus newspaper of UNN then. It read, 'Mr. Transport Delivers'. It left me proud and fulfilled. Unknown to me, the role turned out to be a precursor to an entrepreneurial career in Nigeria's road transport sector.

My point is I did not just wake up one morning and decided I wanted to become a businessman. It was a natural progression of things in my life. Passion, natural traits, flair and interests led me from one entrepreneurial attempt to another. I have always wanted to create or add value. By the time I finished school, it was clear to me that I wasn't going to apply for any job. I had developed confidence in being able to solve problems and earn money doing so. I had built confidence by trying things, failing and then trying new things. As a university student, I went to people's houses to borrow money for business. I once went to someone and said, "Look at my ticket I want to go to Italy to buy things to sell. Can you give me a loan? I will pay you back when I return." The man responded, "Okay, come back tomorrow morning." I returned there the following morning only to be told that he had gone out. The next day he was at home, but he said to me, "Come back tomorrow". When I did, I was informed he had travelled. He kept deceiving me and I never got that money from him. It was massively frustrating. But that's human nature in business. I learnt that when I was about nineteen years old. Some will learn it at twenty-five and some others at thirty five but one just has to learn it at one time or another for business. Such lessons helped to build my confidence in interactions and negotiations.

The Signs Are Always There

I think any experienced entrepreneur who met me as a young man would have found it easy to deduce that I could go into business in the future. I had curiosity, passion and the aptitude for commerce. But having natural abilities or flair is usually not enough. We get shaped and influenced by the world around us and I repeat, it is 'different strokes for different folks'.

I don't really know what influenced me and set me on the path of business. My parents were self-employed, but they never really traded. I simply had a knack for it, I guess. I just followed my instincts. I am Igbo and people say that Igbos are naturally inclined towards business. I am not sure how big a factor that is but I know I have seen many people from different tribes go into business and succeed.

People have also insinuated that the Nigerian Civil War could have had something to do with why people like me who were kids during the war became enterprising. Maybe that is because desperation to survive during and after the war forced us to search for innovative ways to live. I'll give you one example. Immediately after the war, everybody was in fear because the Nigerian soldiers had occupied everywhere and were constantly patrolling. If they heard even the sound of a goat bleat, they would take the goat. So, our work in the mornings was to go and tie the mouth of the goats to make sure they didn't make any sounds. We would then release and feed them in the evenings.

My father didn't join the Biafra Military Force during the war even though men were conscripted in. Maybe, being an ex-soldier, it was easy for him to use his influence in the army to avoid that. But he did play a prominent role in the war. He took care of Biafran soldiers in terms of providing medication, feeding and generally giving support. He did that despite the incredible challenges posed by the war. It was hard on him and all of us. We resorted to farming and I remember always going with him to the farm as he rode on the bicycle that had replaced the car he lost during the war.

We saw real poverty, desperation and hardship during those days and such periods tend to encourage enterprise. The war forced us into rice farming and that meant developing all the disciplines that went with it like waking up early, working hard, harvesting and selling. These are all useful in business. Trying to survive, certainly sharpened us.

So yes, in considering how certain people like me end up in business, one's background and past experiences play crucial roles in either exposing natural entrepreneurial traits or developing them. But we must not limit the range of experiences that can shape a young person's life. For one person, it could be trying to survive a war. For another person, it could be an entrepreneurial parent. For yet another, it could be a case of being influenced by an admired entrepreneurial mentor. So whatever leads to it – family background, a war or a mentor - you need a mindset of enterprise to get into and succeed in business.

Right People, Wrong Roles

As a CEO for many years, I have had to be involved in numerous recruitment related interview sessions. I have also had many parents come in to see me with their sons or daughters, wanting to find job openings for them. This usually makes me engage the young men and women in conversations to know where they could fit in. Many times after those interviews and recruitment related chats, I realized the young man or woman was completely wrong for the job being applied for. For instance, the young man who applied for a customer service job was more fitted for strategy while the young lady who applied for an accounting job, should have been applying for marketing. The young man who wanted to work as an office administrator, was cut out to be a field worker while the young lady who wanted to go to the field was perfect for the available behind-the-scene desk job

.

Many times, I have interviewed entrepreneurs looking for boring desk jobs. For such people, I always try to get them to consider the option of starting their own businesses or taking up more entrepreneurial roles within our organisation. There have been some who told me, "But I have no money to start anything". And there have been times when I said something like, "Okay, if I give you N200,000, what are you going to do? What are you going to give me?" I got responses like, "I have nothing but a laptop" and I responded, "Okay, go and bring your laptop and prepare a document for the loan". The young man would go, return with the laptop and a document which we would both sign and then I would hand over the money and laptop. What I usually achieved was to get the young person ready to risk what he or she had to pursue a business goal. That's important in business and anyone who can do that is set for the big league.

My interviews have also shown me that not every young person out there is cut out for the business world. Entrepreneurship is not for everybody and we need to realize this in a country like Nigeria where entrepreneurship is often promoted for jobless young people as an alternative to earning a living through a job. We should remember that the jobs some are creating, others must manage. The challenge is to be able to recognize who has a flair for business and who does not.

To succeed as an entrepreneur:

You need passion for commerce

You need a sense of curiosity

You need a willingness to create value

You need persistence

You need a sense of innovation

You need drive to succeed.

Name FRANCIS NNEJI

Reg No. 78019009

Dept. ZOOLOGY

Post DIRECTOR OF TRANSPORT
STUDENTS' UNION

Address

Signature

Valid: From Nov 1980 to Nov 1981

As a university student, not only did I get involved in business, I participated actively in campus politics and was elected as the director of transportation for the student union. Many years later, I would start and run a transport company.

In my early twenties after pioneering Rapido Ventures

❦

I was very much involved in businesses while I was a student at University of Nigeria, Nsukka and it paid off later because those experiences I had laid a good foundation for my future as a businessman. I believe our younger years offer us opportunities to explore, to try things and to be enterprising. I also believe that a university should not just be about academics but also about extra-curricular activities that help young people develop holistically.

Are entrepreneurs born or made? That's a question people will keep asking but I believe it's a combination of both.

❦

CHAPTER THREE

--------◄►◄►◄►--------

Everyone Pays a Price

"The question is: what price,
are you willing to pay?"

A reality of actualizing any dream or reaching any target in life is that you must pay a price. The question is, what price are you willing to pay? For me, the price for becoming an entrepreneur and growing in business, has been personal comfort and I believe this is the same for most other people. The extent to which personal comfort is sacrificed is often directly proportional to your level of success as far as the goals you have set for yourself are concerned. In business, I really cannot see how anyone will succeed without giving up personal comfort. You receive what you put in. That fine thinker, James Allen, put it more lucidly when he said:

"There can be no progress, no achievement, without sacrifice, and a man's worldly success will be in the measure that he sacrifices."

I have met with many iconic people in different fields and their examples validate the notion that if you are not willing to sacrifice your comforts, you will hardly achieve success. If you want to build a business, you need to invest time in studying, building relationships, trying out ideas, providing leadership to your team, negotiating and executing deals. You can't do that if you are constantly sleeping, socializing or watching television. Yes, it is fine to do those things but building a business successfully means you will have to drastically cut down on pleasures.

It's like wanting to develop an athlete's body. You can't do that eating every nice-looking food you see. A table with bread, butter, sausages, eggs, beef and all sorts of tempting delicacies might look good but someone training to be an athlete must live with a strict diet while investing in enormous amounts of sweat, energy, and time working out. He must give up the natural urge to eat everything that looks tasty.

Building a business is always about making choices in other areas of life. It's about deciding on how to spend or invest your time. Watching TV, sleeping, partying, and generally indulging in pleasures are things we can't spend too much time on when we are supposed to be building a business. Are they bad in themselves? No. But we always have to make choices about what we are willing to give up for success.

When I look back, from my earliest days in business to more recently, I realize I have always given up a lot of my personal comforts to be able to learn, grow and succeed. After starting Rapido Ventures, I was the last one to buy a colour television among my friends. It just wasn't a priority for me. As money came in trickles, I invested it back into the business. As the business grew, even though I could afford a few luxuries, I often felt compelled to re-invest any extra money in the business. As a young man, I always had friends who came to stay over in the small apartment where I resided. Very early in the mornings, while my friends slept, I would wake up, have my bath and head out for business. Did I feel like sleeping more? Oh yes, I did. Did I prefer staying back home for a few more hours? Oh, yes. But I always felt I had to get moving to survive and that time was ticking away.

When you have such a mind-set, you tend to sacrifice much of your personal comforts to achieve your objectives.

I'll give you another example. One day during the early months of Rapido Ventures when we were dealing in flipcharts, I went to Port Harcourt with Ngozi, my wife, to explore how I could get a metal fabrication company to make panels. Unfortunately, the man in charge insisted that he couldn't solve the problem for us that day and that I needed to return the following day. Ngozi and I had just gotten married and didn't have enough money to pay for a room in a good hotel so if I was thinking of personal comfort when that guy said we had to wait, I would have rather returned to the coziness of our modest home with my new bride. In pure convenience terms, it certainly would have been better to travel about 84 km back home than endure the potential discomfort of a sub-standard hotel room. But the business instinct in me kicked in. If I decided to return home, I was going to pay extra on fuel for the journey and run the risk of not meeting up with the appointment. That didn't seem like a smart business option to me so instead, we found a very cheap hotel and stayed back in Port Harcourt despite the unpleasantness of doing so. I had Ngozi, my wife, to thank for that. If she did not understand the wisdom in paying the price in the short term for benefits that could come later, she probably would have nagged and forced us to return home that evening. Like so many other times throughout my business life, her support made paying the price easier.

Ngozi, a daughter of a top civil servant and chartered accountant of the old Anambra State Government, had been part of my enterprising efforts from my third year in the university when we became close friends. Therefore, decisions like the one we had to make in Port Harcourt that day, were not strange to her. She had seen me make such choices in the past during our school days up till the time we got married. She was used to them. Nevertheless, it was always a testament to her supportive disposition that she went along with me in such instances rather than oppose. There is no doubt in my mind that having a supportive spouse is a significant advantage in business for anyone.

When I started Rapido Ventures, I was just 23 years old - the age of partying you might say. I mean, if people want to paint the town red, you wouldn't be off the mark to guess they would be doing so at 23. My age mates at that time were having fun, going around town, organizing or attending parties.

I hope you are not getting the impression that I was a young man who was too serious to enjoy the attractions of youth. That would be a wrong impression. I went out with friends, enjoyed sports and went to parties during some weekends. We had lots of fun together. We did things young people of our generation did. But none of those stopped me from waking up at 5am and running out to do business.

I don't believe we should lose our friends because we are trying to build a business. I still created time for my friends despite being desperate to use time well when it came to building my business. My friends knew the kind of person I was and with time, they started to respect me for my values. Some of them started saying things like "If you tell Frank, you already know what his response will be." I was fine with that since it meant they knew what I stood for. Throughout the years of building my businesses, I have kept friends because I consider friendship to be important. The same goes for my family. I got married in 1987 when I was 27. I married Ngozi, my school sweetheart, and doing so at such a young age meant

I had little time for romantic relationships while developing my business. Marrying relatively early was one of the things that helped me avoid distractions.

I think I was fortunate to understand the merits of delaying gratification early in life. I knew I had to give up some fun and sleep for my business to grow. I knew I had to delay buying a nice stereo or a colored television for things to move. My neighbors at a point in time asked me what happened to my window curtains or window blinds and they were surprised when I told them I had none. It wasn't that I couldn't afford curtains but buying curtains would mean being short of funds to execute a deal. It was that simple in my head. I needed to give up things in the short term for my business to grow and succeed in the long term.

I believe that as much as I wanted to add value and succeed, I was also driven by a fear of failure. My first office cost me N760 for ten months. The building was owned by the family of a lawyer called Barrister Kamalu back then. When I negotiated the space with him, I appealed to him to take payment for ten months. He agreed and pulled out his receipt.

"Give me the money", he said. I handed it over to him, he collected it, counted and turned back to write on the receipt. Without looking up, he asked, "What do I write on the receipt?"

"Rapido Ventures" I said.

He paused, looked at me and asked, "What's your actual name?"

"Frank Nneji" I said.

He turned back to write on the receipt, signed on it and handed it over to me. The receipt read, 'Frank Nneji, trading as Rapido Ventures.'

That was ten months of rent paid and a receipt signed by a lawyer. I suddenly became afraid of failing. What if I put up a signboard outside of the office and really got started and failed? What if I took the full plunge and messed up?" I thought about how I could end up being the subject of jokes.

During and immediately after my National Youth Service Corps year, I lived with an uncle who had some other boys constantly visiting him. One of them was an artist and I appealed to him a few times to help me design a logo for

Rapido Ventures. The guy kept trying different designs and he eventually came up with one I liked. He never collected money from me for his efforts.

Later, I moved into my own apartment and one day he came around for a visit and saw me packing. "Frank, where are you going?" he asked. "I am not sure this is going to work at all. I am going back to my village", I replied. The guy fell on the ground and laughed hard.

"I thought you had Rapido Ventures. What about all the logos we have been designing?" he asked, reeling with laughter. He didn't know I had rented a two bedroom flat somewhere in the neighborhood and was moving on. That occurrence got me thinking about how people would laugh at me if I failed. I wasn't ready for such ridicule. In a way, I dreaded it. Many people who succeed, are driven by the fear of failure rather than the hope for success.

Many young people don't understand that they have to give up much today to get a lot tomorrow. Nowadays, a young entrepreneur will do his first job, make some money and then embark on a spending spree. How is he going to make his business grow if he keeps spending money he is supposed to re-invest in his business? In 1989 when I bought our office complex in Owerri, it cost N30,000. I had to pay in installments. What was in vogue at that time were the Mercedes Benz cars known as 'Flat Boots'. Very decent used ones were being shipped to Nigeria and sold to people who mostly wanted cars as status symbols. Driving a Mercedes Benz indicated 'success'. I could have spent the money I had buying a car that would make me look like someone who had arrived, but it made more sense paying for the complex to grow the business. It was a no brainer for me. I reckoned that if I worked hard and smart enough, I would be able to get a good car later.

A Popular Story: The Struggling Butterfly

A man found a cocoon of a butterfly. One day a small opening appeared. He sat and watched the butterfly for several hours as it struggled to force its body through that little hole. Until it suddenly stopped making any progress, and looked like it was stuck.

So the man decided to help the butterfly. He took a pair of scissors and snipped off the remaining bit of the cocoon. The butterfly then emerged easily, although it had a swollen body and small, shriveled wings.

The man didn't think anything of it, and sat there waiting for the wings to enlarge to support the butterfly. But that didn't happen. The butterfly spent the rest of its life unable to fly, crawling around with tiny wings and a swollen body.

Despite the kind heart of the man, he didn't understand that the restricting cocoon and the struggle needed by the butterfly to get itself through the small opening were God's way of forcing fluid from the body of the butterfly into its wings to prepare itself for flying once it was out of the cocoon.

-Narrated by Dan Western

I don't know if this story is true or not but it's a common one told to remind us how struggles and sacrifices are important for our development and success. Our struggles in life develop our strengths and without them, we never grow and never get better.

Succeeding in business
requires sacrifice.

There is always a price to pay
to build a business.

The greater the price you pay, the
higher your chances of succeeding.

Unless you give up some comfort and
pleasure, you are unlikely to succeed.

Comfort is perhaps the biggest obstacle
for many young people planning to go
into business.

As much as you must give up much to
succeed, you need to be balanced.

Don't lose your health or
family because of business.

I met Ngozi while we were both students at UNN and we got married in 1987. My example and so many others I have observed, convince me that having the right spouse can be a massive advantage in business. Ngozi's support and wisdom have helped me to navigate through the complicated world of business.

PART II

THE ABC TRANSPORT
STORY

CHAPTER FOUR

The Birth of ABC Transport

*"Don't chase money. Create value and
money will follow"*

This might sound like an old, unrealistic and silly cliché but take it seriously because it is smart advice: *don't make money your primary pursuit in business.* Let me clarify that. It doesn't mean you shouldn't have making money an important objective in business neither does it mean a desire to make profit in business is wrong. On the contrary, a business that fails to make profits on a consistent basis, will fold up soon enough. What that advice means is that making money should be a result, product or consequence of solving problems for others. Money comes when you offer good products or services. Think about it. You go to certain restaurants to spend your money because they offer you good food, comfortable environments and helpful services. You spend your money paying for electricity because it powers your house appliances. You pay a petrol station because the petrol they sell to you power your car which moves you around. That, of course, assumes you use a petrol powered vehicle. Think about anyone you pay money to. It is always because of something you get back in return. People ask me every time, "What inspires you in business?" I tell them the same thing, "I always want to create value. Every time I have been successful at creating value, I have made money one way or another". If you focus too much on money, you will likely get into trouble. That's a reality I have discovered.

Today, ABC Transport is a publicly quoted company that provides road transport services operating through coach passenger operations, sprinter passenger operations, shuttle passenger service, haulage services, cargo services and others. The coach passenger operations segment provides long distance service using luxury buses. The sprinter passenger operations segment includes long distance service using midi buses. The shuttle passenger service segment provides shorter distance service using mini buses. The haulage services segment consists of long distance haulage servicing manufacturers. The cargo services segment comprises of cargo services including mails and light. The hospitality CTI segment includes budget accommodation targeted at sleep-over passengers.

ABC Transport has over 1,500 employees who work for a brand with incredible growth possibilities. But how did the business start? Did it begin because I was looking for money or I wanted to make more money than everyone else? No, it didn't. It was a mindset for creating value that birthed ABC Transport.

The Beginning of ABC Transport

Sometime in 1991, I was in a bus going to Lagos from Owerri. The journey was very uncomfortable and eventually the bus broke down along the way. While all of us passengers were upset and worried, I got thinking about the situation. How come people couldn't travel comfortably and safely by road across Nigeria in commercial vehicles? How come people couldn't get the best services possible while travelling in commercial vehicles? What if someone could offer much more than just taking people to their destinations via commercial buses? I began to ponder on the situation and as is often the case when an idea is forming in my head, I started to narrate a story mentally. The story was about a bus company that would be on schedule; that would provide comfort and safety for travelers; that would be driven by professional, uniformed drivers; that would serve snacks and drinks on board and that would compete with the airlines. It was an exciting thought. Placed within the context of the existing road transport industry that lacked such buses and services, it seemed like a no brainer in terms of how it could attract passengers willing to pay extra money to travel in comfort. The idea took over my mind. It was about creating value and solving a big problem. Money was of course, going to follow. I had no doubts about that, but money was not what occupied my mind then. I had been running a successful business for about nine years prior to that day. Rapido had grown to become a market leader so in a way, you could argue that I had no reasons to be thinking about something else.

But a real-life situation got me thinking innovatively about the road transport business. I saw an opportunity to create value and I was hooked on doing that. Entrepreneurship is about adding value, solving problems and providing products or services that make life easier and better for people. Whether it's Henry Ford's obsession with making cars more accessible to the masses, John D. Rockefeller's pursuit of easily distributing refined oil through a network of pipelines, Bill Gates' dream of providing easy access to personal computers run by operating systems with Graphic User Interfaces or Aliko Dangote's drive to supply every home with essential food commodities, entrepreneurship has always had solving problems and creating value at the core of its definition.

After I became taken by the idea of moving people around in comfortable and safe buses across Nigeria, I began to learn everything I could about the road transport business. I asked questions, observed and pondered. I studied the local bus operators as much as I could.

At the stage when I was collecting information for the new business, I found my younger brother, Jude Nneji, very helpful in researching and documenting all the available relevant data we could find. Jude, who currently works with ABC Transport Plc as a deputy managing director, has always had a knack for such things. He garnered experience in his school days as a member of the editorial team of his department's magazine. That was when he horned his reportorial skills.

Jude documented all our findings on the road transport business and was constantly on the lookout for new information on the Industry. That helped me tremendously in understanding the state of the industry.

Professor Pat Utomi of the Lagos Business School captured the story of the road transport sector in Nigeria well in a 1997 LBS paper titled, 'Thriving in Niche Markets':

> "Many of the founders of Nigerian transport companies were people who had been in the motor spare parts trade or who had worked for vehicle owners rising through the ranks from conductor to transport manager, before establishing their own companies. The major ones had considerably large fleets and were equipped with large service and maintenance workshops. The largest transport company in the country, Ekene Dili Chukwu Motors, had a fleet of over 1,000 buses. The norm for Nigerian transport companies was for the drivers to receive relatively low salaries, the expectation being that income would be made up from other sources. An important source of income for the drivers was the provision of 'attachment seats': improvised seats in the gangway that were occupied by roadside passengers who paid

lower fares. Preachers and medicine sellers were also allowed access to the buses for a fee. The conductors were usually employed by the drivers rather than the company to maintain a good working relationship."

About the time when I was pondering on starting ABC Transport, there was a magazine back then called, *Business* that once featured an article titled, 'The Motor Park Millionaires'. The article profiled the major transport operators in Nigeria at that time. Of course, almost 99% of them were from Anambra State, mainly Nnewi. I grabbed that magazine, read it and began to demystify the road transport industry. It featured companies like Izuchukwu, Ekene Dili Chukwu, C.N. Okoli and the rest of them.

I read every other thing I could find. That's something I have always done for every business I decide to go into. I create a file, label it and put everything I can find about the business in it. Things are much easier today. You only need to go online to research on anything imaginable.

At a point in time, I started going out in the mornings to where the other buses picked up passengers just to study how things were being done. I developed a rapport with a young man called Chima, one of the managers of a bus company at the park. Chima helped me to understand how things worked at the pickup points. I remember an incident when their big 'Oga' came around. I stretched out my hand to greet him but got a suspicious look in response. "Who is this person?" he asked, almost with disdain. Chima said, "Oh, he's my friend". The man paused, looked at me again for a while before he finally decided to greet me. Chima later worked for me and that boss of his, many years later, visited my office to seek for help. His business had crashed and he was desperate to revive it.

You must understudy existing businesses if you are planning to go into any sector. The things I saw, while studying the existing companies, strengthened my resolve to pursue my vision. The industry clearly needed the services I was proposing.

After becoming confident about the viability of the business I wanted to start, I developed a plan to raise money for a few buses to get it started. I began to approach potential financiers to tell them the story in my head and paint the picture of what could be if such a bus company existed. "I am going to create a bus service that will always be on schedule, provide snacks on board, carry only the right number of passengers and have uniformed drivers who show respect to the people they drive", I told them.

"Have you done this type of transport business before?", one of them asked me.

"No", I responded.

"Okay, those buses you want us to finance, where are they made?" he asked.

"I want to start with Hiace Buses. They are made in Japan" I said, not knowing where he was going with his questions.

"Fantastic! So, please tell the Japanese to also get you the drivers who will not only drive but also offer the other services you are talking about", he concluded in the most sarcastic and cynical way possible. He simply did not believe my idea was going to fly.

But that did not discourage me. I kept searching for a financier until Diamond Bank, a relatively new bank Rapido Ventures had been doing business with, finally agreed to fund ABC Transport based on a N1.5m operating lease agreement. We were in the same building with a company called WESTEX, a Japanese agency and we approached them to get us Toyota Hiace buses at discounted costs. This turned out to be a smart move. Diamond Bank consigned the purchase to WESTEX and we eventually got the buses at N320,000 each. That was a good rate in 1992.

Diamond Bank's funding paid for five of those buses while I bought the last one. Earlier, when I went to the bank to make a case for the loan, they had asked what was going to be my contribution to the startup capital. I told them I could afford to buy one of the six required buses and we agreed they would pay for the other five.

After we got the buses, I put curtains in them, branded them and put the ABC Reindeer logo on them. The choice of logo had a lot to do with the fact that my wife and I were zoologists.

I bided my time with the buses. ABC Transport was going to be launched at the appropriate date and it was going to focus on delivering the services I had dreamt of. Before the takeoff date, some people kept nudging me to use the buses to make quick money especially during the Christmas season when people travelled a lot in Nigeria.

But I refused to lose focus. I knew exactly what those buses were meant to do, and no one was going to make me change course. I told them, "I am planning something different, setting things up for a new business and training people for that."

ABC started operations in February 1993 with six Toyota, fourteen seater buses. The early months were exciting. I was implementing ideas, printing tickets that looked like airline tickets back then and advertising in creative ways. Our unique selling point was comfort and safety. We approached the Federal Road Safety Commission (FRSC) to train our staff. We put them in uniforms and made sure we took off on schedule every day. At the start, we never had enough passengers because we were new and charged premium. Occasionally, just two or three people would be in a bus before we took off because we always insisted on leaving on time. After doing that for a few weeks, our drivers came to my house one early morning, woke me up and said, "Oga, this is not how to run a transport business o. This venture is going to fold up soon if we don't change how we are running it. How can we be carrying only three passengers all the way to Lagos yet you insist on not stopping along the way to pick up more passengers? What if we make stops, pick up more passengers and pay you a percentage of money collected in such instances?"

I said, "I don't want it that way. This business is different, and we need to stick to the plan. Meanwhile what is your problem? I agreed to pay you an allowance and salaries. Am I not doing so?" "But Oga, this thing won't last the way we are going" one of them responded. "Leave that to me. Just go back to work", I said. They did go back to work with a lot of doubts about the viability of the business. Some of them were even convinced I could have been involved in shady deals to be getting the money I was using to run the business despite not having enough passengers.

People will always tell you why or how an idea will never work. You must be careful not to get discouraged or lose faith in what you are doing. If I had listened to those skeptical financiers or those drivers, things could have turned out very differently. Three months after we got started, the buses started getting filled up. Some more months down the line, the buses were getting fully booked twelve days in advance and that was despite the fact that we were charging premium for comfort and safety.

From inception, we offered drinks and snacks on board. The buses did not have 'attachment' seats and neither preachers nor hawkers were allowed except they were coming in as other passengers. When the buses broke down, passengers were entitled to a refund of a proportion of their money at any of the stations on presentation of their tickets. The amount refunded usually depended on where the bus broke down.

1993 was very good for the business even though it was tumultuous for Nigeria due to the annulment of the 'June 12' elections. Moshood Abiola, popularly called MKO Abiola of the Social Democratic Party (SDP) had defeated Bashir Tofa of the National Republican Convention (NRC) in a presidential election that was generally judged to be free and fair. International observers stated that there had been no evidence of the violence and vote-rigging that marred the last round of balloting in the previous Nigerian elections held in 1983. Nevertheless, the election results had been delayed due to some legal challenges in courts, especially the lawsuit brought on behalf of a group of rich businessmen, military officers and politicians called the Association for a Better

Nigeria (ABN). The association claimed that the 1993 elections had lost credibility because of vote tampering and corruption. The association won a court order restraining the National Electoral Commission (NEC) from releasing final results. It was that court order that the ruling military government led by Ibrahim Babangida, used as the basis for annulling the 'June 12' election. What followed was anarchy. Riots broke out particularly in the South Western part of Nigeria. Rumours that the election was annulled because MKO Abiola was a Yoruba man began to spread and ethnic tensions became apparent. People started to travel in thousands, afraid that the violence breaking out in major cities like Lagos, could escalate and erupt into another Civil War. It was against this backdrop that ABC Transport suddenly became faced with the challenge of too many demands for travelling tickets. It was a classic case of how a bad situation could have a positive spin on a business. The few buses we had couldn't cope with the traffic movement so it became obvious that we needed to expand early into the business. It was like having no choice, we increased the fleet by getting four more buses.

In March 1994, we obtained two, 55-seater Volvo luxury buses under a N6.5m operating lease agreement with Diamond Bank Limited. Each bus was equipped with TV and video for on board entertainment during travels. In addition, every baggage checked into the luggage compartment was tagged for proper identification. We also had an accident insurance scheme and every passenger was covered by Personal Accident Insurance Policy. We introduced the ABC Gold Card which we gave to frequent passengers on the ABC buses. A gold card holder is entitled to a seat on any bus any time he or she came in.

In 1995, we acquired two Volvo buses under a lease agreement with Commercial Bank Credit Lyonnaise. We got three more buses in 1996 and another three in 1997. The 1996 acquisition was financed by Diamond Bank and the 1997 acquisition was financed by Fidelity Union Merchant Bank. We stopped using the Toyota buses sometime in 1996 because of high operating and maintenance costs.

The term of the leases we got was typically fifteen to eighteen months and the charges on the facilities averaged 40%.

The lease rentals were usually huge cash drains and to service the debt obligations, we had to find ways of enhancing cash flow beyond revenues from seat sales on the buses. A source of income was the sale of space on the back of the bus tickets to companies for advertising. We made an average of N50,000 monthly from that idea. Another source of income was cash transfer and parcel services from one city to another.

I should mention that it was a bit sad that Diamond Bank did not travel all the way with us on our business growth trip. The initial loan they gave us was for about eighteen months. The second loan they gave us came before the tenure of the first one ended. That was a sign they were happy with the way things were going. By the time I asked them for money to buy the luxurious buses, our relationship had developed well and processing the loan was much easier. Those Volvo buses didn't cost more than 5.5 million naira each, back then. But as time passed and the Nigerian economy evolved, Diamond Bank and many other new generation banks seemed to get less interested in taking risks with relatively new entrepreneurs in certain sectors. After some time when I wanted to expand, Diamond Bank seemed to have lost the drive to support ABC Transport even though the business was picking up pace.

The young bankers in the bank kept dragging their feet. I was grateful for the chance they took to help ABC Transport get started but when they began to lose interest, I knew we couldn't afford to move at their pace if we wanted to maintain our momentum. Fortunately, Fidelity Merchant Union Bank got interested in our business. At that time, their managing director was Nebolisa Arah who had brought in innovation and energy into the young bank. They took over the financing for ABC Transport and helped to take the business to the next level.

25 August 1992

The Managing Director
Rapido Ventures Ltd,
122 Wetheral Road,
Owerri.

Dear Sir,

OFFER LETTER

We are pleased to advise that Diamond Bank Ltd has approved your request for a lease finance facility under the following terms and conditions:

Lessor:	Diamond Bank Ltd (The Bank)
Lessee:	Rapido Ventures Ltd.
Amount:	N1,500,000.00 (One million, five hundred thousand Naira) only.
Purpose:	To purchase some buses for use as commercial vehicles.
Equipment:	Five (5) units of 14-seater Toyota Hiace buses (details as per supplier's invoice).
Tenor:	18 months from date of first drawdown (inclusive of three months lease-in-process period)
Commencement:	The lease is to be booked after three months lease-in-process period i.e. three months from date of first drawdown.
Lease-in-process period:	This refers to the three-month period immediately preceding the booking of the lease. During this lease-in-process period, the N1.5 million facility will be treated as a Bridging Finance for the procurement, registration and commissioning of the vehicles. Accrued interest shall be paid monthly in arrears by the lessee.
Pricing:	i. Lease Rate: .0532 i.e 5% above DBL's prime lending rate currently 35% p.a.
	ii. Management fee: N30,000.00 payable annually.

The first and second (displayed on the right) pages of the loan offer letter I received from Diamond Bank to buy the first buses for ABC Transport. It was that loan that set us in motion in 1993.

	iii. **Arrangement fee of N30,000.00 chargeable once and for all.**
iv.	**Legal fees - N40,000.00 ..**
Rental Payment:	15 equal and consecutive monthly rentals of N128,698.71 commencing one month after the lease-in-process period. Rental payments will be recalculated in the event of any change in our prime lending rate.
Security:	i. Legal ownership of the leased vehicle
	ii. Guarantee of the company's Managing Director, Mr. Frank Nneji, supported by his personal financial statement.
Purchase Option:	The Lessee shall have the option to purchase the vehicles at the end of the lease period at a residual value of 5% of the cost.
	This residual value shall be secured by deposits as follows - N25,000.00 before drawdown and N50,000.00 one month after drawdown.

CONDITIONS PRECEDENT TO DRAWDOWN

1. The Lessee must actively operate a current account with the Bank. All cash lodgements from the proceeds of the business will be made at our Victoria Island Branch on a daily basis.

2. All upfront fees, (i.e legal, management and arrangement fees) totalling N100,000.00 must be paid.

3. First instalment of purchase option (i.e. N25,000) to be deposited in a non-interest bearing account.

4. Offer letter to be duly accepted.

5. Execution of a Lease Agreement incorporating the terms and conditions of the offer letter.

6. Receipt of a Board Resolution of the company authorising the acceptance of the facility.

7. Execution of our guarantee form and personal financial statement by Mr. Frank Nneji.

When we got our luxurious Volvo buses we branded them as, 'Business Class Service' and that idea took ABC Transport to a whole new level. The prices we offered to passengers were usually higher than those charged by the other transporters. By July 1997, we charged N890 for the Lagos-Owerri route while other transporters charged N700.

Other companies in the road transport sector started feeling the impact of our presence. They realized we couldn't be ignored. We were becoming a formidable competitor. Naturally, some began to antagonize us and put wrong ideas in the minds of potential passengers. But we were never deterred. We continued to grow. We kept comparing ourselves with the airlines and not the other road transport companies. We looked for travelers who travelled by air occasionally and persuaded them to travel with us instead because we could offer comfort and safety at cheaper rates. We emphasized customer service. We responded to enquiries and reacted to complaints. We collated and managed passenger manifests like the airlines did. We got drivers to apologize to unhappy passengers. If a driver failed to win back an angry customer, he was suspended from work until he won that customer over. We were determined to show that the customer was king. We provided better leg spaces, magazines, fabric seats, onboard toilets, and reclining seats in our 'Executive Sleeper Service'. We worked with the bus manufacturers to specify what we wanted on the buses.

The whole industry was shaken. Competitors had no choice, they simply had to adapt. They suddenly started using tickets like we were doing. It made all the sense in the world. There were special feelings passengers had when purchasing tickets for bus trips. It was a new idea in Nigeria and the whole process seemed very professional. Prior to then, all the passenger got was a receipt after payment. We had also secured terminals where passengers could sit while waiting for their buses. Before then, the practice was to buy a ticket, get a receipt and go inside the bus to sit down until it got filled up. There was nothing like terminals. Our competitors knew that was another game changer and they had to adopt the idea. One of them, a friend of mine, told me that his passengers were putting him under pressure to get them seats. I remember him saying, "Frank na you dey cause all these rubbish o! How can passengers be telling me to buy seats for them when they pay me very little?" I could understand his frustration. I knew we were in the same industry but not exactly selling the same services. They wanted to move people from one end to another, we wanted to give people being moved, comfort and safety. But it gradually became apparent to some of them that they had to change their approach to the business. We had certainly raised the bar and to keep up, they had to adapt. Suddenly, other bus companies stopped carrying extra passengers and some even started giving passengers snacks on their buses. The revolution had started.

I saw the changes competitors were making as things to be proud of. The industry was growing, and Nigeria was better for it. As for ABC Transport, we kept growing and kept looking for ways to be innovative.

We operated mainly on the Lagos-Owerri, Lagos-Port Harcourt routes initially but in April 1997, we expanded operations to three other routes. We focused on executives who had tight schedules and preferred to travel overnight. It helped that we stuck to specific departure times ranging from 7.30pm to 9.00pm. The sleeper service featured reclinable seats, individual reading lights, and early morning coffee and tea. We also began to look at the Lagos – Enugu, Lagos -Kaduna and Lagos - West Coast routes.

As at July 1997, we had 102 employees that included drivers, transport officers (I) and transport officers (II). The transport officers (I) were required to be university graduates and they were usually appointed station managers. The transport officers (II), held Nigeria Certificate in Education (NCE) and Ordinary National Diploma (OND) certificates and were ticketing officers.

Out of the twelve drivers we employed as at July 1997, four had Ordinary National Diplomas. That was a departure from having illiterate drivers which was a common industry practice at that time. Our preference for educated drivers meant we had people who could understand and appreciate our values, handling the wheels. We gave them manuals and handbooks that highlighted what drivers and other operational staff were to do in different circumstances. Because they were educated, they were able to read and understand those materials.

The station staff were paid station allowances in addition to their normal salaries since many of them stayed back in the stations until the buses running the sleeper services left at 9.00pm. We ensured that our staff were appraised four times every year. We also put suggestion boxes in the buses for passengers to regularly tender their complaints. We introduced a "Customer Forum" event where all our customers were invited to make suggestions for the improvement of the company's services.

In those early years of ABC Transport, I had no formal training in business to have learnt the practices adopted by our young company but I was someone who garnered a lot from experiences, observations and personal studies. I was also blessed to have good employees who teamed up with me to build the ABC Transport brand.

Two things are essential in business as far as I am concerned: creating value and making money but the former is more fundamental. I believe it is by creating value that you make money. If you are not creating value in business, then you are not really doing the type of business that will be sustainable. We made money at ABC Transport by creating value. We didn't pioneer the road transport industry in Nigeria. There had been other companies in the business before we got on board. It was already a congested industry. However, the mortality rate of transport businesses was high. Bankers had gotten their fingers burnt investing in the sector before we came in. Many families in Nigeria had tried one form of transport business or another. You always found a retired uncle who attempted to use his car for transportation or give it to someone else to use for the same thing. People tried because they assumed that the transportation business was one that was straightforward in terms of calculating the return on investment. "This vehicle can carry four people at N100 each. That means N400 per trip. If I make ten trips in a day, that means N4,000 per day for me", the average person thinks, forgetting he will buy petrol, maintain the car, pay for toll fares and deal with emergencies.

What we did when we came in was to introduce innovation. We basically created value. When we did that for commuters, they became willing to pay that little extra.

Money follows solutions.

If you create value,
you will make good money.

Curiosity helps you
create value.

Focusing on creating
value means focusing on
the long term.

Innovation is what
can turn a business into
a market leader.

CHAPTER FIVE

If You Have It, Flaunt It
"It's never too early to start branding and advertising"

Anyone trying to build a business absolutely has to invest in branding and advertising and it is never too early to do so. Branding is what defines your business in the minds of customers or potential customers. Advertising is what promotes your brand. Even if you are taking off on a shoe string budget, you should invest something, no matter how little, in branding and advertising. I can't emphasise this enough.

When people have needs, they think of certain products, individuals or organisations that can meet their needs. That's another way of saying they think of certain brands. If people want to travel by air, they think of Virgin Atlantic, British Airways, Lufthansa, Emirates Airline and others; if they want football, they think of the English Premier League or La Liga; if they want luxury fashion and leather goods, they think of Gucci or Versace; if they want reliable mobile phones, they think of Samsung and if they want world class university education, they think of Harvard. In Nigeria, Vitafoam means mattresses and Close-Up means toothpaste. That's the power of branding.

What you want early in the life of your business is for people to connect it to specific needs they have. You want them to think of your business when they want certain solutions to certain problems and no matter how limited you are in terms of funding, you have to start doing everything possible to position your brand in their minds.

When we started ABC, we wanted it to mean *safe and comfortable road transportation* that could be compared to the airlines but we had the challenge of getting people to buy into that innovative idea. Our new company was revolutionary in the sense that it was trying to introduce completely new ways of operating a road transport business in Nigeria. To complicate things a bit, our innovativeness required us to charge customers rates significantly higher than what the existing bus companies were charging. We were promising comfort and safety equal to what people would get on airlines and that meant we could not stick to the popular rates. We stood the risk of being described as expensive.

It was a new direction with clear target customers in mind: people who wanted the comfort, safety and class of air travel but would be happy to pay less and travel on road if they could be guaranteed the same benefits the airlines offered. To reach this set of people, we had to find creative ways of reaching them and the conduit for that was advertising. But what is notable here is that this effort started very early in the business. I didn't wait to have a lot of money to make it top priority, neither should anyone else who starts a business.

Determine the Best Medium to Advertise Your Brand

One of the most important things a business must do is to determine its best channels for advertising. This is so, not only because advertising budgets are normally limited but also because if a business does not use the right channels for advertisement, it will fail in reaching its primary market targets.

Back in the 1990s and early 2000s, newspapers were the most common channels for advertising in Nigeria. The online media options we are used to today were almost non-existent then. Few people and organisations had access to the internet and of course we had nothing like Facebook, Twitter, Instagram or Whattsapp at that time. So the challenge was how we were going to reach people and sell our innovative ideas to them.

We explored multiple options including sharing handbills at places like churches and on the streets. But our top options were newspapers, radio and television. It's important to remember that the television and radio spaces in Nigeria had not experienced full liberalisation so the options in those spaces were considerably fewer than what we have today. So, even though we used radio and television to advertise, our primary channel was newspaper.

Our objective was clear: convince people through innovative products and services and via creative adverts to opt for road travels rather than the airlines. I knew that every advert had to be specific, precise, effective and creative. I made the creation of those adverts a primary responsibility of mine. In a way, that was inevitable because I have always had a natural flair for coming up with marketing ideas and also because as the one who ran the business, I had a good overall view of our operations and a vision of where we were going. I think leaders of any business should be involved in developing marketing, advertising and branding concepts for the business. These are too important to be ignored because they end up determining the perception outsiders have of that business and as you probably know, perception is often everything in business.

I come up with 80% of advert ideas at ABC Transport. Till today, I write many of our advert scripts. Sesan Oyebode of Novitas Advertising (formerly, Resnova Advertising) has always been my reliable sounding board and co-creator. From the first day of ABC Transport until now, his company has handled ABC Transport's creative projects. Sesan has an understanding of where we are coming from and where we want to go. Anytime I come up with an advertising idea or script, I send it to him and his team would analyse, critique and offer supporting suggestions to make the idea better before we run off with it.

Brand Them All

When I refer to branding, I do not just mean that of a company. I also mean branding of each product and service you want to offer to people. Each one must be branded and advertised. This is the way to imprint them on people's minds. To gain market advantage, appeal to the class of people we were after and make a case for our 'expensiveness', we kept creating new services and products for ABC Transport and for each one we created, we worked hard at branding and advertising it.

Some of the brands we created include:

- ABC Transport Tours
- Executive Express
- Coach West Africa
- ABC Petty Cash
- Shuttle Service
- SprinterPlus
- ABC Hauls
- Charter Service
- Super Sleeper
- City Transit Inn

Each one needed its own market space and it was our duty to create those spaces for them in the Nigerian and West African markets. Creating those spaces meant branding and advertising to a very large extent. We gave each one a logo and a unique identity.

Let me share some of the adverts we published in newspapers in the 1990s and early 2000s. My objective here is to hopefully get you to see how we kept innovating and using advertisements to promote those products and services.

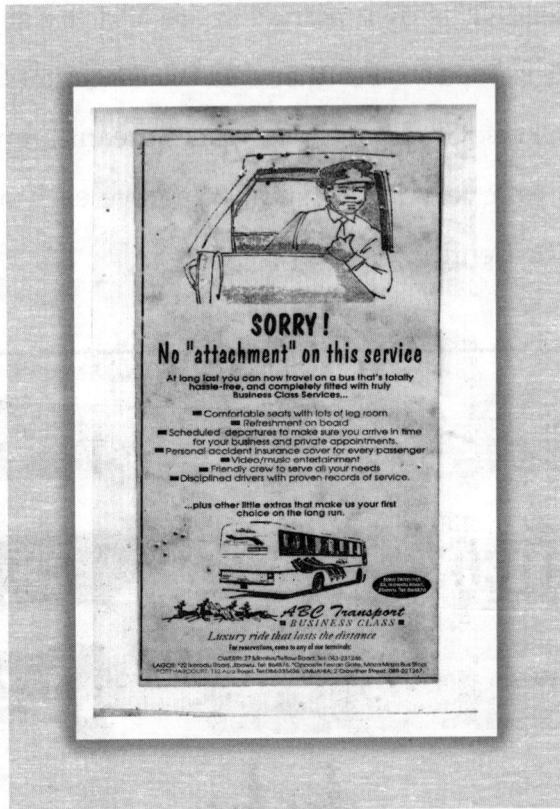

SORRY!
No "attachment" on this service

At long last you can now travel on a bus that's totally
hassle-free, and completely fitted with truly
Business Class Services...

■ Comfortable seats with lots of leg room.
■ Refreshment on board
■ Scheduled departures to make sure you arrive in time
for your business and private appointments.
■ Personal accident insurance cover for every passenger
■ Video/music entertainment
■ Friendly crew to serve all your needs
■ Disciplined drivers with proven records of service.

...plus other little extras that make us your first
choice on the long run.

ABC Transport
BUSINESS CLASS ■
Luxury ride that lasts the distance

Sorry! No 'Attachment'

One of our earliest promises to customers was never to allow
for 'attachments' in ABC Transport. 'Attachment' was a term
used to describe extra passengers on a bus carried by greedy
drivers. Back then, drivers had the culture of always overloading
the buses with people thereby endangering lives and or
inconveniencing passengers. The idea was to make extra money
for themselves. If a bus could take thirty people for instance, the

driver adding 'attachments', could pick up ten extra passengers ('attachments'). When reporting back to the bus or business owner, he would not account for those extra passengers hence keeping the money they paid for himself.

It was the normal practice in the industry before ABC Transport started and it was one of the most discouraging factors for people who wanted to travel comfortably. Many of such people avoided travelling by bus simply because of 'attachments'. It is worth mentioning here that the inconvenience of 'attachments' was one of the things I experienced on that bus trip from Owerri to Lagos that got me thinking about starting ABC Transport. It was even perhaps the most significant factor that led to the ABC thinking. That particular bus was overcrowded, noisy and it eventually broke down on the way. I found the trip almost unbearable and perplexing. Something needed to be done.

When ABC got into the road transport industry with the promise of 'comfort' and 'safety', it was obvious to us that we could not allow that culture of overcrowding buses in our organisation. We decided to let potential customers know about our decision thereby assuring them that travelling with ABC was going to be a comfortable experience for them. So we designed advertisements to drive this new standard. The 'No Attachments' advert became one of our first campaigns and it was significant in making ABC Transport a unique brand.

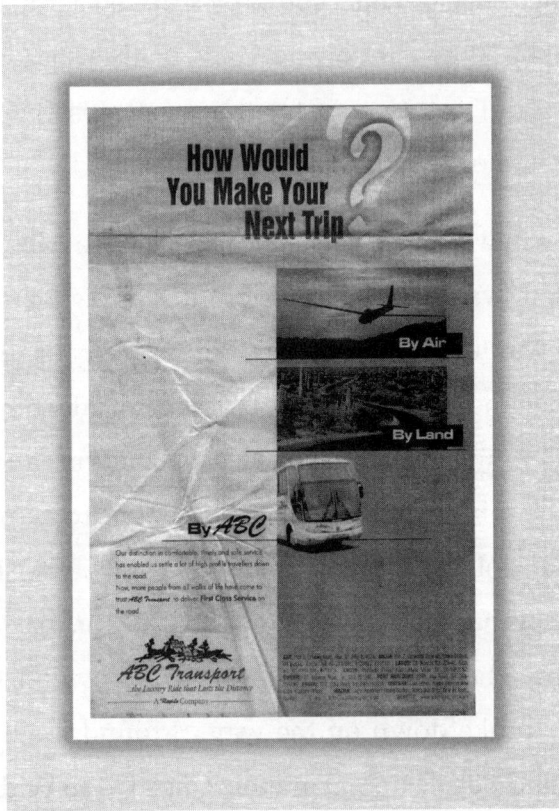

How Would You Make Your Next Trip?

By Air

By Land

By ABC

ABC Transport

By Air, by Land, by ABC

One of the challenges we had was convincing those in our target market to travel by road. We had to make strong cases to make them comfortable about the idea of travelling by road rather than air. So we came up with this advert campaign, *'By Air, by Land, By ABC'* to hint that ABC was something between travelling by air and by land; something that was an improvement on usual land options.

The Road is Getting Better

Of course Nigerian roads were in a deplorable shape back then so a campaign like 'The Road is Getting Better' was bound to catch people's attention. The advert was never about the state of Nigerian roads but about how travelling by road with ABC was going to be an improvement on road travels for any customer. Again this was about making a case for road travels with ABC.

How Well Do You Know Your Country?

In coming up with innovative ideas that would appeal to our target customers, we thought it would be interesting to inculcate an internal tourism angle in our services and appeal to patriotic instincts in Nigerians. The reality was that not many Nigerians really knew Nigeria in a geographic sense. So "Why not get to know more about your country by travelling on road with us?", we asked. This advert got many people thinking about the idea. With us, they could actually get to see more of Nigeria. They knew we were big on comfort and safety and that further made the idea more appealing. This is another example of coming up with an innovative idea and using advertisements to promote it.

Pound Foolish, Penny Wise

In the 1990s, getting on a plane in Nigeria used to be tough. The airport terminals used to be overcrowded with people scrambling to get tickets for short local trips and agents used favouritism to sell tickets to passengers. Yet, tickets were very expensive. That situation presented ABC Transport with an opportunity. We decided to pose the questions: "Why suffer so much to get on a plane if you are paying a lot to get the tickets? Why don't you travel with us instead and pay less while you are assured of comfort and safety?" Given the condition of the airline industry in Nigeria at that time, those were reasonable questions to ask and they got people thinking.

Even though we were considered to be more expensive than other bus companies, an important selling point we had was reduced costs within the context of serving as an alternative to air travels. We were certainly cheaper than the airlines. The common saying is, 'penny wise, pound foolish' but in the advert in focus here, you can see how we switched it to 'pound foolish, penny wise' for creative effects and also because our aim was to give air travelling passengers a less expensive alternative.

This advert highlights how we offered a solution to a problem and directed advertisements to it. It also points to the fact that adverts need to be creative for them to be captivating.

The Sleeper Service

Night travels has always been a popular global practice for many years. People have always liked to travel comfortably at night and arrive at their destinations in the morning, ready to do business. During the late 1990s, night travelling by road gradually became popular in Nigeria because security had improved on the roads. But the problem back then was that the issues of inconvenience on buses discouraged blue collar workers and middle class citizens. Traders on the other hand were typically rugged people who were used to travelling in those inconvenient conditions so they were the ones who mostly patronized the existing bus companies.

We decided to change that situation by finding a way to convince people they could travel in comfort at night. Whenever you want to do something differently or introduce an innovation, you have to 'brand' it to create a convincing impression in the minds of your potential customers. When we got in, we branded our own night travelling operation, 'Sleeper Service'. We told potential customers that it was a special night travelling service that guaranteed comfort and safety.

The 'Sleeper' in our campaign, meant you could sleep conveniently as you travelled with us at night. If you wanted to travel at night, sleep comfortably while doing so, get to your destination the following morning feeling very fresh and ready for business, then ABC Transport was your best option. It was a classical case of leveraging on the power of branding.

The 'Sleeper Service' got off to a good start and appealed to our target customers. But we were determined to improve on it. When we started getting complaints about leg pains, we came up with what we called the, *'Super Sleeper'* service. This ran between Port-Harcourt and Lagos and the buses for it had fully reclineable seats but had no air-conditioners.

We then came up with the *'Executive Sleeper'* service which ran between Lagos and Abuja. This service had all the basic configurations of the Super Sleeper option plus additional benefits like air-conditioners and much better reclineable seats. The idea was phenomenally successful. People loved it and soon we struggled to cope with demand.

The adverts we designed drove these services. We ensured each advert sold the benefits of the ideas to attract customers. Charging as high as N7,000 while others were charging N2,000 and N3,000 became insignificant because people could see the extra value we had brought into the market.

What is most notable here is how we kept improving on the night travel services and how we distinguished each new service. Each stood as a brand and meant different things to our customers. Aligning our advertisements to this helped a lot in making those services and brands successful.

Introducing

A 5-Star hotel on wheels

Whether you choose to travel by our super luxurious business class buses or our air conditioned mini-express bus service, you'll get your favourite first class treatment while you journey smoothly to keep your vital appointments.

☐ Comfortable seats with lots of leg room
☐ Refreshment on board
☐ Scheduled departures
☐ Roomy luggage space
☐ No 'Attachments' or stop overs in transit
☐ Disciplined drivers and Security escorts

Plus NICON PERSONAL ACCIDENT INSURANCE COVER

Travel by ABC and enjoy luxury that lasts the distance.

For reservations, come to any of our terminals:
OWERRI: 27 Mbaise/Tetlow Road. Phone: 083-231246.
LAGOS: Opposite Festac Gate, Maza Maza Bus Stop, 13 Western Avenue, Ojuelegba.
PORT HARCOURT: 112 Aba Road. UMUAHIA: 2 Crowther Street. 088-221267

ABC Transport
Luxury ride that lasts the distance

"If toilets are in the airplanes, why can't they be in our buses? If airplanes are cool, why can't our buses be cool? Why should passengers be travelling while suffering the heat of tropical weather?" Those are questions we asked before deciding to put toilets and air conditioners in our buses. Again, these were new in the road transport industry in Nigeria and they were selling points in our attempt at appealing to our target customers. Once we implemented the ideas, we designed this '5-Star Hotel on Wheels' advert and went to the newspapers to let potential customers know they could indeed get comfort whenever they travelled with ABC Transport.

Terminal 3

Another innovative idea we brought into the road transport industry in Nigeria was the creation of proper bus terminals. Remember we had our eyes set on the airlines and we wanted to compete with them. If airlines had terminals, why couldn't we have terminals? Before we got into the industry, waiting passengers would just hang everywhere enduring all sorts of inconveniences until their buses were ready to depart. When we came into the industry, we decided that to deliver on our 'comfort' and 'safety' promises, we needed to build terminals where passengers could sit comfortably while waiting for departure. The Amuwo-Odofin terminal was our third terminal in Lagos. Our first modern terminal was in Abuja and the second was in Owerri. We got creative when it came to the Amuwo-Odofin Terminal by using 'Terminal 3' in advertising it. The backdrop to that was the newly launched 'MM2' Airport in Lagos. It was widely referred to as 'Terminal 2' and was growing in popularity. We thought that an advert with a 'Terminal 3' headline was bound to catch people's attention and it sure did. We simply rode on the popular slogan of the time.

In making adverts, you want to be relevant and creative. Those are sure ways of catching attention.

But What About the Budget?

My thinking when ABC Transport started, was that it was suicidal from a business perspective, not to have an advertising or branding budget for any business. I still think so today with the benefit of hindsight. No matter how lean it is, you must create a budget to promote your brand and advertise your services. People won't spend money on your business if they don't know about it and no one will pay for a service he is unaware of. If your budget is lean, make sure you spend the little money you have smartly. Pick the right advert channels and always ask the right questions: How can we get maximum exposure with this small budget? What is the best medium to use to reach out to our target customers?

In the case of ABC Transport, I knew we had to stretch ourselves and spend money on advertising. It was tough but we had to do it otherwise, how else were we going to get people to know there was a new company and a new idea in town? We fitted our adverts into our budget but doing that always requires creativity.

One of the things I did was to engage in barter arrangements with some media houses. In exchange for moving their staff or products like newspapers around the country, I got airtime or advertisement slots in newspapers and magazines. In such cases, we saved money while reaching out to our target customers.

I also cultivated excellent relationships with the motoring press. I got ABC to do things like taking some of them along for our maiden trip to Accra. We went with all the motoring editors of Vanguard, Champion, Sun and other Nigerian newspapers. Through that, we developed good rapport and it was subsequently easier to get them to publish any information we had that their readers could find useful. Over the last twenty years, I have developed good relationships with some of them like Joel Opara and Frank Kento. This has helped in some ways in keeping our advertising, branding and marketing budgets manageable.

Whatever your budget is, ensure you find the advertising that suits you and go for it because like I said earlier, it will be suicidal from a business perspective, not to advertise at all.

It is suicidal not to brand or advertise your business

Branding defines your business in the minds of customers.

Advertising is what promotes your brand.

Not having enough money must never be an excuse for not branding or advertising.

Don't wait until your business is big, start branding and advertising now.

Let your advertising be relevant and creative.

Reindeer

---·-·◄◦○□○◦►-·---

We picked the Reindeer as the symbol of ABC Transport and created our logo based on it. My wife, Ngozi, and I, made that choice due to our background in biological science, we understood, perhaps more than most others involved in the business, the relevance of the Reindeer as a symbol of many things ABC Transport represented. Ngozi once published an article (displayed on the right) she wrote about that incredible animal in ABC Transport's quarterly magazine, *Reindeer, which* is the longest running on board transport magazine in Nigeria.

STRONG, FAST, UNITED ...

THE REINDEER STORY

BY NGOZI NNEJI (MRS)

The symbol for which the Associated Bus Company Limited, operators of ABC Transport, is known and from where this magazine derives its name is an intriguing one. Reindeer is an animal that has many peculiarities. It is strong, fast and moves in the association of fellow reindeers.

The Reindeer is a mammal of the order of cross-check (Even-toed hoofed mammals). It comes in various sizes. While many of them have antlers or horns on their heads, male reindeers have solid limy antlers on their heads. These antlers are shed and grown afresh each year. Their legs are usually long with two (rarely four) functional toes on each foot.

They belong to the family of carvidae (deer, etc) and are also called (Caribou Rangifer). Arctic deer are domesticated in some polar regions, ranging from Spitsbergen and Scandinavia to Eastern Siberia. They are also found in North America where there are two types: the northern or barren ground Caribou of the Tundra and Taiga, and the Woodland Caribou of Canadian forests. These two are game animals cherished for meat, hides and antlers. The third type known as Mountain Caribou, is regionised by sportsmen.

Reindeer differs from all other deers in that both sexes have antlers. However, those of the females are smaller and simpler. The antlers are long with moderate branching on both main beams and forwardly pointing brow tines. The Reindeer weighs as much as 300kg and stands 0.7-1.4m (2.3-4.6 feet) at the shoulder. The small domesticated races are about the size of donkeys. They are stockily built and have large literal hoves which allow the feet to spread on snow or soft ground. The skin cover is thick and consists of hard, brittle outer hairs covering a dense underfur.

These animals are strong swimmers, always found in herds, an attribute which the Associated Bus Company Limited seem to have

A reindeer

adopted so well. ABC Transport moves in association (like The Reindeer) with the passengers. The Reindeer is famous for seasonal migration between the summer and winter ranges. They breed in fall during which two calves are born after gestation of seven and half months. The staple food for this animal is a lichen popularly called the Reindeer Moss, which the animals reach by scraping the snow away with their feet. In summer, their diet includes grasses and saplings.

Reindeer moss (Cladonia rangiferia) is a fructose (bushy, branched) lichen found in great abundance in lands. It is an erect, many branched plant that grows up to 8cm high, covers immense areas and serves as pasture for reindeer. Its periods of most rapid growth are spring and fall when high humidity and cool temperatures prevail.

The main enemies of reindeer are humans, wolves and lynx. The reindeer of the lapps is kept as pack animal for its meat, milk, and hides used in tents, boots and clothing. In Siberia, the reindeer is also used as pack animals and as mounts.

Company News

ABA GETS *EXECUTIVE EXPRESS*

Concrete arrangements have been finalised for the introduction of the Executive Express Service to the commercial city of Aba. This service which has been operational on Lagos, Abuja, Port-Harcourt and Owerri route is the most recent introduction in the dynamic services of ABC Transport. It offers a lot of luxury yet unheard of in the Nigerian road transport industry. The Executive Express features fully air-conditioned buses, deluxe seating with extra leg room, cold bar and in-built toilets, while spotting all the perks for which the company is known. Courteous crew, Insurance cover, entertainment and refreshment on-board or available in this service.

ABC transport came into Aba in 1995 with the business class service and captured the taste and interest of the populace. Relationship between the company and the Aba passengers/community has been mutually beneficial and consistent except for a few months of break in operations observed by the company in order to relaunch a standard service. ABC transport has since resumed full operations in the commercial city and will soon complement it with the introduction of the Executive Express Service.

CHAPTER SIX

How We Attracted Equity Investment

*"You can grow your business through debts or
by giving up part of it for funding"*

The road transport industry in Nigeria, has always been a fascinating, challenging and competitive one, more so in the early 2000s. There were many issues to deal with and like in many other industries, we had instances when business had to be reviewed and directions redefined while putting multiple factors into consideration. For example, modern buses were equipped with engines that had technology and electronic controls, so maintenance staff had to possess relevant technological skills. Sadly, there was scarcity of skilled manpower able to keep buses in good condition. Also, our industry was getting saturated. Although dominated by many small operators that owned between one and thirty buses, there were over seventy registered road transport companies and about 1,300 high capacity buses making up their fleet size. There were also many other matters like the fact that Nigeria's new democracy brought in attempts at instituting new policies and laws that directly or indirectly affected the way we were running business. Any business person will tell you that one of the most important things for business growth and stability, is consistent or predictable public policies and laws.

But business can be strange. On one hand, you could be experiencing unprecedented growth in terms of brand acceptance, popularity and even revenue, while on the other hand, you could be facing industry related challenges that threaten the future of your organisation or its overall capacity to expand from a long-term perspective. As a business person, you need to be able to observe all these dynamics of your business and industry. You need to be able to assess things properly and make the best judgements for the benefit of your business. You cannot run any business well if you do not constantly study the socioeconomic contexts within which it is operating.

The early 2000s was a period like the one I just described for ABC Transport and the road transport industry in Nigeria. The renowned Professor Albert Alos, formerly of the Lagos Business School and Professor Olufemi Bamiro of the University of Ibadan, in their important book, 'The Pains and Gains of Growth', observed the following about the road transport business and ABC Transport:

'...the total yearly revenue for the year 2001 was estimated to be N22 billion. The six largest operators controlled about 47% of the market. In 2002, ABC Transport was ranked 6th in terms of fleet size. The company however was reputed to be the most innovative and premier road transporter in Nigeria. Because of its emphasis on professional management and passenger care, ABC charged slightly higher prices than most of its competitors. The unrivalled infrastructure it possessed – like its terminals, transit inns and superior buses – was a major factor in the continued loyalty of its clientele. ABC's focus on creating customer loyalty was part of its strategic intent. Reputation for reliable, safe and timely service allowed the company to build loyalty and trust (and to charge a premium for it). ABC believed that this strong loyalty was a deterrent to prospective entrants to the industry.'

The authors captured the situation perfectly. We were receiving awards. The Chartered Institute of Transport and Logistics, Nigeria, judged us to be the Best Transporter of the year 2002. The Traveller Magazine named us the Best Inter-state Land Transporter in 2001. FATE Foundation named me the Model Entrepreneur of the year. Those were all good but they didn't take away the realities and challenges of our industry.

Ifesinachi Transport, Chisco International Limited and Cross Country were examples of companies that were catching up with us in the areas we had defined as our strength. Passengers started feeling they could get cheaper rates from them while also receiving quality service. That pushed us on though. We became more aggressive in innovation. We tried to diversify and move to unchartered territories while maintaining our primary focus. We introduced the cargo delivery service as a service for passengers with excess luggage, which was transported separately by truck. The service developed into a consolidated cargo delivery system. We introduced a cash transfer service which was a personal message service for ABC customers who relied on ABC to send small sums of money to friends and relations in destinations where we had offices. We introduced the City Transit Inn which provided overnight accommodation for ABC passengers. We also held majority equity in ABC Express Courier Limited (Abex Courier), which was a fast-growing courier company with strong domestic coverage nationwide.

This is what you do in business. You create new product and service lines as competition increases. You are consistently innovative. There is a reason why Apple always follows up an iPhone 5 with an iPhone 6 and then an iPhone 7 and so on. There is a reason why Samsung always comes out with new models of their phones every year. There is a reason why Honda, Toyota, Ford and all the major car brands, change something in their cars and release new models annually. It's called innovation. It's what you must commit to doing in business on a constant basis.

But despite all the new ideas and lines of services, we were not distracted from the core objective of becoming the undisputable leader in the road transport business. We began to think about how to make this happen. We developed a plan to build a standard terminus and workshop to improve our capacity to handle additional fleet from Lagos and increase revenue from cargo. We decided we should replace old vehicles so as to keep the maximum fleet age of three and a half years and we also decided it was time to start exploring markets outside of Nigeria.

It was clear that we would need a lot of money to make those plans work. I started to dream about competing globally and attracting capital market investments. Despite our growth, our reliance on local banks had saddled us with debts and paying back was becoming increasingly tough not just for us but for other companies in the industry because things were getting worse in the country. Roads were deteriorating badly and that was affecting maintenance costs significantly. As anyone with a vehicle knows, when you drive regularly on bad roads, all sorts of problems pop up in your vehicle no matter how rugged it is. This was affecting profit projections of companies in the business. I knew we needed to raise money but I also knew the type of money we needed was not going to come from banks. Banks had started to classify the road transport business as highly risky. They became extremely reluctant to give out loans to companies like ours. It was therefore becoming more difficult and expensive to rely on banking facilities for working capital. This naturally got me thinking about raising equity capital to finance the expansion of ABC Transport.

Many business owners or entrepreneurs make the mistake of wanting to rely entirely on their own financial resources to either start a new business or expand an existing one. While I am not saying this can't be done or is a bad idea, I believe it is smarter to always have an eye for what some will call OPM (Other People's Money). You can get money from different sources to start or expand a business. Money you use for your business tends to be categorized in terms of the consideration (payback) you must give in return for it. But basically, it is either debt or equity. How you go about getting either this debt or equity is what some will refer to as 'raising capital'. Debt means taking a loan while equity means selling part of the ownership of your business in exchange for money to run it more effectively. Some sources of money for a business tend to come immediately to mind: high-net-worth individual investors (e.g "Angels"), financial institutions and funds and equity offerings (e.g., ownership interest offered for sale to investors), such as private placements and public offerings. However, there are other sources of money. These include your friends and family, vendors, customers (through advance payments), and government lending programmes or grants.

The ABC Example

At the beginning when ABC was about to start, I relied on bank loans to fund the purchase of our initial buses. At the point, in 2002, when banks were reluctant to give loans and it was tough to service such loans when they were given, raising equity investment looked like the sensible thing to do and so I began to pay attention to potential equity investment partners. I found and settled for a company called Capital Alliance Nigeria (CAN). CAN was an investment and advisory company established to promote private sector-led investments in Nigeria and West Africa. By 2002, CAN had access to over USD 35 million available for investment. CAN emphasized three factors in their investment strategy: the achievement of a 30% IRR, the quality of the company's management and an equity participation which represents close to 40% of the company's value.

I thought ABC Transport fitted into the type of companies CAN was looking for but I needed to know if CAN would want to take on ABC Transport, so I met with Okey Enelemah, one of the founders of CAN, and had an extensive preliminary conversation with him about the possibility of them buying equity from ABC Transport.

Okey had heard about me and ABC Transport's progress. He felt we were exactly the type of organisation CAN would like to invest in. He was a very thorough man, so he went about getting every scrap of information he could get on ABC Transport and the men behind it. He got references from suppliers, banks who had given us loans, customers we had served, and just about everyone who had dealt with us in any way.

I believe Enelemah and the CAN team were impressed with ABC Transport. Our company was performing well, we were diversifying intelligently and since CAN wanted a company generating good cashflow, we seemed to fit in perfectly into their profile. Our ability to generate good returns on their investment was too attractive to ignore despite whatever risks were there. Enelemah certainly saw the possibilities and the signs looked good. We agreed to have a formal meeting with CAN sometime in March 2002.

Ahead of that meeting, I was anxious. I wanted the deal to go through. Everything I saw in ABC Transport's future seemed to hinge on being able to raise enough money to execute the plans. I had been clear about what we needed to do, now it was time to raise the money to make things happen. I was of course worried about the few things that could mess up the deal. We dealt with the ones we could control and simply resigned to the fact that CAN would decide on the ones we couldn't control.

I got the presentation ready and got set to do what might end up being the most important deal in the life of ABC Transport. On D-day, I felt the burden of the significance of that presentation, but I also had a quiet confidence that things might work out since we had gone that far. I presented our expansion plans and why we needed CAN's investment in ABC Transport. They seemed impressed. After that meeting, we had subsequent ones and had to open our books and doors to CAN. That is never an easy thing to do but a necessary one when contemplating bringing in shareholders. Fortunately, we had nothing to hide as we had developed a culture of doing things properly right from the start.

The decision to go for equity financing was one that I took

carefully. I prefer to think things through before making decisions especially if the decision is a major one. Maybe it has to do with the fact that once I have made up my mind, I commit whole heartedly to the decisions made.

The entrepreneur or business owner who is thinking about exploring equity finance must avoid being emotional – something a lot of Nigerian business owners tend to exhibit when it comes to giving up total control of their businesses.

Many fail to appreciate the fact that bringing in partners can provide immense leverage for growth, a sense of accountability and pressure to deliver results. I realized all these and knew that the best way to push ABC Transport to that level I wanted was by opening up to equity investments.

Of course, there are repercussions to embracing equity investments – especially when you do so and under perform. With equity investment, you lose some control and, founder or not, you can be fired if things start getting really bad for the business. I knew these risks, but for me, they were potential prices to pay for growth.

We kept meeting with CAN after that initial session and each time, I went prepared with my management team. I also took along advisers from Fidelity Bank which had been supporting us with loans up till then. This is something the entrepreneur must learn to do. It is not smart to go to meetings unprepared especially if the meeting is a negotiating one or if it is as important as the type of investment meetings we were having with CAN. The business owner must also never be reluctant to hire or use professional advisors or consultants. Whatever you don't know, get someone to make up for your shortcomings. It might cost you in the short term, but it will be worth it in the long term.

As we kept on discussing with CAN, my hopes for a positive outcome, increased. I had desired for a long time, that getting ABC listed on the Nigerian Stock Exchange (NSE) would not only provide us with the opportunity to grow in leaps and bounds but would also provide opportunities for our staff to become shareholders of ABC and create a stronger sense of belonging while allowing me to disengage from the business when the time became ripe.

I also thought it would change the perception of the company's ownership and management profile. Like I said elsewhere in this book, I think it is important for employees to know that the business is bigger than the founder and his family. This helps to build commitment and loyalty. I wanted ABC staff to see the company as being beyond Frank Nneji. I wanted them to see that the dream was bigger than me and that it was one they could plug into in the long term. I knew that though the idea of the company was originally mine, external strategic advice and additional capital could help improve the operations of the company and lead ABC more securely into the future. It was with such a mindset that I pressed on in our discussions with CAN which elaborated on its willingness to exit the joint ownership arrangement in five years and support the idea of going public.

CAN wanted to engage an independent reputable firm to conduct due diligence on ABC and a reputable law firm to perfect the legal agreement. They asked me to pay the cost of both. I agreed to pay half of the cost and, if the deal went through, pay the other half later. KPMG Professional Services was eventually hired, and the firm conducted the exercise.

Fortunately, KPMG's report put ABC Transport in good light and further reassured CAN about our worthiness. CAN felt more comfortable about investing while the five-year duration of investment gave me a breath of assurance. I felt that with the arrangement, if things turned out badly, we could have a private sale of the investment or a public listing of shares.

ASSOCIATED BUS COMPANY LTD						
FOUR YEARS FINANCIAL SUMMARY						
As at 31 December						
		1996	**1995**	**1994**	**1993**	
		N'000	N'000	N'000	N'000	
FUNDS EMPLOYED						
Share Capital		1000	1000	1000	1000	
Profit and Loss Account		37,314	19,859	5,345	2,282	
		38,314	**20,859**	**6,345**	**3,282**	
ASSETS EMPLOYED						
Fixed Assets		81,914	55,627	38,247	5,212	
Net Current Assets/(Liability)		{43,600}	{34,778}	{31,912}	{1,940}	
Deferred Assets			10	10	10	
Net Assets		**38,314**	**20,859**	**6,345**	**3,282**	
TURNOVER & PROFIT						
Turnover		101,866	60,733	19,667	5,535	
Profit before taxation		21,465	17,622	3,941	2,835	
Profit after taxation		17,955	14,513	3,063	2,835	
Dividend		{500}	_	_	_	
Earnings per share	N	17.9	14.5	3.1	2.8	
Dividend per share	N	0.5	_	_	_	
Dividend cover	N	35.9	_	_	_	
Earnings & dividends / share are based on shares of N1 each for all yrs &						
profit alter taxation for earnings.						
NOTE: The company has only operated for four years.						

ASSOCIATED BUS COMPANY LTD		1996		1995	
STATEMENT OF VALUE ADDED					
As at 31 December					
		1996		**1995**	
		N	%		%
Earnings		101,865,738		60,732,503	
Cost of brought in goods and servicees		36,102,757		18,417,109	
		65,762,981	**100**	**42,315,394**	**100**
DISTRIBUTION					
EMPLOYEES		5,829,982	9	2,966,486	7
GOVERNMENT (TAXES)		3,510,513	5	3,109,361	7
FINANCE PROVIDERS					
Interest		15,290,555	23	7,773,335	18
Dividends		500,000	1	_	0
MAINTENANCE OF ASSETS					
Depreciation		23,176,905	35	13,953,309	33
Profit re-invested		17,455,026	27	14,512,903	34
		65,762,981	**100**	**42,315,394**	**100**

*Before I ever thought that we would one day ask an investor to come in, we had developed the habit of keeping our books well. The above financial reports are examples of how we ensured we kept tab of our finances year in, year out. One of the most important things to do for a new business, is to keep proper records and books. I promise you, it will pay off one day.

ABC Transport's negotiations with CAN took eleven months. After the first few meetings and three months into the deal, a Memorandum of Understanding (MOU) was drafted and signed by both parties. That document outlined how CAN would work with ABC to add value to the business and increase profit, institutionalize systems, recruit effectively and assist in pre-Initial Public Offering (IPO). The MOU also specified that a new Board of Directors would be constituted, and that both parties would have the right to nominate directors to the new board pro-rata to their shareholding.

Another significant thing about the MOU was that it stated clearly that CAN would provide the new Chief Financial Officer (CFO) for the restructured ABC Transport. That was understandable because investors like to keep track of their investments and ensure that the business is well run while generating substantial profit. One way of ensuring this is by hiring a good CFO. However, after various interactions with our team, CAN was impressed with our CFO and decided that there was no need for a change.

Dick Kramer

Let me round up this chapter by mentioning Dick Kramer, a remarkable character in the private equity transactions with CAN. Dick is a brilliant American gentleman who arrived in Nigeria in 1976 to start Arthur Anderson. That initiative led him to becoming an iconic figure in Nigeria's business community and the role model for many contemporary business consultants and leaders in the country. Dick co-founded CAN as a private equity and venture capital firm specializing in expansion capital, management buyouts, turnarounds, and start up investments.

I met him during ABC Transport's interactions with CAN for investment. His influence on my life and business, turned out to be critical in a very positive way. I remember the mind shifting meetings I used to have with him at his house in Lagos. Dick had a way of getting you to expand your horizon; to think big while being pragmatic. In discussing ABC Transport's direction, he brought his vast knowledge of the Nigerian economy to bear. Though American, he had become, very much a Nigerian. He understood the Nigerian business landscape better than any other person I had ever met.

Apart from the core issue of equity investment in ABC Transport, Dick played a mentoring role for me during those meetings we had. He was excited about the prospects of ABC, especially in logistics and he felt that I was not exploring the possibilities well enough. My sessions with him turned out to be eye opening and they led to ABC Transport going more into cargo logistics which is now a major part of our business. Back then, cargo was less than 5% of our business but now it constitutes about 30%.

A business can be financed through debt or equity investment.

Debt indicates loans with clear pay back timelines and interest rates.

Equity investments indicates selling part ownership of your business often to a financier.

To take a business to the next level, most business owners go for either debts or equity investment.

If you are not ready to lose some control, your business will often stagnate at a particular level.

Work hard at doing things right from the start. You may need to open your books to someone, one day.

You must always be ready to pay for good specialists and advisers.

Growing a business, bigger than yourself, motivates employees to commit fully.

DICK KRAMER

CHAPTER SEVEN

------◦◦◦◦------

Swimming with the Sharks:
Corruption, Ethics & Integrity

"Can You Run Business Successfully in Nigeria Without Being Corrupt?"

Running business within an environment and culture of corruption is very difficult and unfortunately, that is what you experience in Nigeria. For a young business entrepreneur, this could become a dilemma because while you want to maintain a certain level of moral standard in business, you will discover that some people and organisations are unwilling to engage you if you don't play ball with them. No matter how good you are, you will realize that meritocracy means little and what matters is how willing you are to 'grease palms'. This can be extremely tough for any young entrepreneur who wants to maintain a strict moral code or ethics in business in a country like Nigeria where people want their own share from profits

WHO SAYS YOU CAN'T?

they have not even made.

As a young entrepreneur, I was faced with this challenge a lot. There were many times when I battled with guilt because I felt forced into situations contrary to my moral and ethical standards. This book is, in many ways, about helping others with my story and to do that, I have to be as plain and open as possible. Like any other young entrepreneur operating in Nigeria, I faced the monster of a system full of corruption, and people who cared little about moral or ethical codes in business or life generally. Many times, people will blackmail you into doing things. Nigerian police officers do this often. For instance, you are stopped at an illegal checkpoint and despite not committing any driving offence or having all your car papers up to date, they find every ridiculous reason to delay you simply because they want a tip. Imagine heading to an important meeting when that happens. Imagine being late for a deal when that happens. This is a reality of doing business in Nigeria.

Fortunately for ABC Transport, despite being a road transport company and driving all over Nigerian roads, we have been fortunate not to experience being forced to bribe police officers at checkpoints perhaps because our buses are branded, and our reputation became strong early in the business. I think police officers that stopped our buses had the perception that we were well connected and that we could easily have them reported. Our corporate image helped a lot in giving us some respect on roads. People knew we were a premium brand and that we could communicate easily with high end people and that we were influencing policies with our brand. But this doesn't mean there have not been times when a few policemen went to the extreme of attempting to force us to bribe them.

I had my own fair share of experiences. When I was supplying educational materials to institutions and government parastatals, people demanding for bribes was a big problem for me. I would get the job done but someone would refuse to release my money except I agreed to pay a percentage of it to him. The procurement system for institutions was terrible back then. But things improved during the Olusegun Obasanjo Government. The insistence on due process and the strengthening of the Bureau for Public Procurement (BPP), made things a lot better.

There were also times when we had to fight to be treated fairly because others who were willing to give bribes were given contracts ahead of us even though we were obviously better qualified. We have sent petitions to the BPP to insist on certain cancellation of contracts because the recipients of those contracts cheated to get them by giving bribes. We forced the hand of the government to deny bids given to unqualified companies who were trying to manipulate the system through bribes, to get contracts ahead of more qualified organisations. Of course, when you do that, you are treated with coldness by the civil servants in the government unit involved. Your chances of getting contracts reduces drastically because you are seen as the party spoiler. When you decide to do such things, you have to be realistic about how people will perceive and treat you. Many have lost contracts and deals because they refused to play ball with blackmailers or give bribes. It's a price to pay in most instances like that. This is why doing business in Nigeria can be really tough for anyone determined to stick to clear moral and ethical codes in business.

Bribing has become so much a part of our corporate and institutional systems that business can be extremely difficult for organisations whose primary clients are institutions and government parastatals. Usually, someone within the system who has a say in whether you will get the contract or when you will get paid, will pose as a stumbling block to you until you grease his or her palm. They often have clear ways they communicate the conditions for you. The experienced business person usually gets the message on time. The neophyte usually learns quickly after a few frustrating experiences. Those who are willing to play ball, get the contracts or get paid quickly. As for the more 'principled' organisations, the impact of the delay tactics deployed by their blackmailers can be devastating.

The thing about kickbacks and bribes is that they eat deep into your profits. This is one of the reasons why I grew frustrated with the business approach of Rapido Ventures. It got to a point when I knew that I couldn't cope with the constant demands and blackmails from civil servants we were supposed to provide products and services to. It was clear that we had to change our strategy in terms of marketing and who to make our primary targets. We started to focus on supplying dealers rather than the government directly. Even though this cut down our profit margins drastically, we found it to be a much better approach because we no longer had to deal with constant requests for kick-backs.

As a businessman, I often ponder on the devastating impact of corruption on businesses in Nigeria. I am not sure it has dawned on us yet but it is perhaps the deadliest disease destroying lives in Nigeria. I cannot begin to outline the negative effect of corruption on businesses in Nigeria. In 2017, the National Bureau of Statistics (NBS) released a result of a corruption survey in the country. The survey was conducted in collaboration with the United Nations Office on Drugs and Crime and the European Union who were keen on finding out about the quality and integrity of public services in Nigeria and the impact of corruption on daily life in the country. Premium Times reported the public-sector findings of that survey in an August 2017 publication:

"According to the NBS, the estimated value of bribe paid to public officials by Nigerians in a year is N400 billion.

> *'Taking into account the fact that nine out of every 10 bribes paid to public officials in Nigeria are paid in cash and the size of the payments made, it is estimated that the total amount of bribes paid to public officials in Nigeria in the 12 months was around N400bn, the*

equivalent of $4.6bn in purchasing power parity,' the report stated.

"This sum is equivalent to 39 per cent of the combined federal and state education budgets in 2016. The average sum paid as a cash bribe in Nigeria is approximately N5,300.

"This means that every time a Nigerian pays a cash bribe, he or she spends an average of 28.2 per cent of the average monthly salary of N18,900," the NBS added.

According to the survey, in a year at least 82 million bribes were paid to public official. Furthermore, it revealed that of the 52 percent of Nigerians that had contact with public officials in that period, no fewer than 32 per cent of them paid or were asked to pay a bribe.

The study also revealed that cash is overwhelmingly the preferred form of bribe with 97.3 percent of respondents saying officials made direct request for cash. Food and drinks comes in distant second with 1.4. per cent followed by exchange of other services of favour (1.1 per cent) and valuables (0.8 per cent).

According to the NBS, 94.2 per cent of those who made direct request for bribe asked for cash, 4.2 per cent asked for food and drinks, 1.7 per cent requested for exchange of other favours, while 0.9 per cent asked for valuables.

The Nigerian Police is by far the most corrupt public institution, according to the survey. The survey revealed that that the frequency of bribery was more among police officers (46.4 percent). Incident of bribery in the judiciary comes at a close second after the police with prosecutors and judges flagged as being among the most corrupt. Prevalence of bribery among prosecutors is put at 33.6 per cent, and judges/magistrates at 31.5 per cent."

Some will even argue that the figures above are too low and that the situation is far worse. I shudder to think about it. We are losing jobs, innovation, creativity, meritocracy, incredible profits and even lives to corruption in Nigeria.

As Rapido Ventures and ABC Transport grew, I had to get more involved in international partnerships to bring in products and services to Nigeria. This was difficult because no one trusted Nigerians. Every foreign company we approached was sceptical about doing business with us simply because we were Nigerians. Do you realize how humiliating and frustrating it always felt? Can you imagine what it would mean to Nigeria if the world trusted us in terms of the kinds of opportunities we could suddenly begin to have?

An example is an experience we had with a company called Telex Communications in Minnesota. They were experts in making cassette duplicators back in the 1980s and 1990s. When we initially wrote Telex Communications, we were ignored. They simply didn't want to have anything to do with us. After about a month, we called them, and someone said to us, "Yes, we got your letter, but we don't do business with Nigerians" I had to write them again to persuade them to reconsider us, but they still did not respond. I didn't give up. I called them again and asked why they were discriminating against all Nigerian companies. I told them we were different, and they wouldn't regret dealing with us. They eventually agreed to give us a try but only on the condition that the transactions were purely on cash basis. I found it ridiculous, but we had no choice. Fortunately, we were able to develop that business relationship and prove to them that Nigerians were not the thieves they thought we were. When that business relationship grew, they came over to visit us in Nigeria, to see for themselves the things we were doing. I also made several trips to their office in Minnesota over time. Trust grew between us and their perception of our country completely changed.

That was one of many examples. We could have easily missed doing business with Telex Communications and so many other companies, especially those from Europe and America. They had all believed that every Nigerian and by extension, every Nigerian company, could not be trusted. Our reputation had gone bad. Things got worse particularly in the early 2000s when some young Nigerians became famous for internet scams. They were popularly known as '419ers' and later as the 'Yahoo, Yahoo Boys'.

These boys became extremely skilled at advance-fee scams which typically involves promising the victim a significant share of a large sum of money in return for a small up-front payment which the fraudster requires to obtain the large sum. Once the payment is made by the naïve victim, the fraudster disappears or continues to come up with extra fees that the victim must pay to get the transaction to finishing point. The bait is usually a loan, contract, investment, or gift.

This form of scam messed up Nigeria's reputation globally. The country's name became synonymous with it and invariably, with scams and crime. For those of us who wanted to do legitimate businesses with foreigners, the situation became our nightmare.

Another related problem was when people representing their companies, came to buy things or services and asked us to mark up the prices for them. For example, if the normal price was N1,000, they could ask us to make it N1,500, get paid N1,500, and then return the extra N500 to them. When Nigerians channel their creativity to making money by any means, it's incredible the type of ideas they come up with. It was always a messy situation for us whenever people asked us to mark up our prices and give them the extra money. We had to come up with ways to solve the problem. First, we set limits on how much mark-up anyone could ask us for and then we came up with the idea of giving them discounts rather than mark ups. With the discounts, they could earn the money they wanted.

There are many things in the Nigerian business environment that go contrary to one's ethics but to survive, you have to look for a way around them. You have to be creative and find solutions without contradicting your ethics or breaking the law. This is imperative for any young business entrepreneur. The target must be to gradually build a reputation for honesty and integrity. It will always be tough, but it must be done. Once people – foreigners or nationals – know you as a person of integrity, it will become a lot easier to have their trust for business transactions. I believe this is one of the most important things an entrepreneur must achieve – to become known for integrity. This is something that opens doors, attracts businesses, brings helpful partnerships and secures the loyalty of talented employees.

Let me share a related observation to end this chapter. I believe retail businesses have more potential than other types of businesses in a very general sense in terms of generating cashflow and profits. Even though they tend to have smaller profit margins per sale, they usually have the advantage of large numbers of buyers or customers. This is a difference I quickly saw between Rapido Ventures (which was more focused on supplying government institutions and private organisations) and ABC Transport, which is largely, a retail business. Perhaps more relevant to the theme of this chapter, is the fact that retail businesses tend to reduce people's exposure to demands for bribes by employees of organisations. In a retail business, members of the public check out your products and services, determine if they meet their needs and simply decide to buy or not to buy directly from you. For ABC Transport for instance, if you like the services on offer, you will simply buy your ticket and hop on board. You wouldn't try to blackmail me before paying the fare for the ticket.

Even though I am not saying that every young person should go for retail businesses, if you were to ask for my advice on the type of businesses with the best prospects for creating wealth and which can also shield you from the temptation to always bribe people, I would say that my personal preference will be retail businesses.

Also, to the young person out there trying to do business in Nigeria or build a brand, you should have clear moral and ethical standards for your business, have a clear conscience and stay within the boundaries of the law. But you should also be pragmatic. Look for solutions to every sticky situation. Idealists don't easily survive in business in Nigeria. Pragmatism is essential.

There is no substitute to ensuring that your brand develops a character with integrity, honesty and high quality even though you might be functioning in a corrupt business clime. Your company culture must not be known for corruption. Therefore, endeavour to get things right early on in your business. When KPMG was sent by CAN to check our books, they were impressed with how well we had been doing things. One year earlier than then, we didn't know an external body was coming to assess us, so it was not a case of cleaning things up for assessment. We had simply instituted corporate governance from the onset, developed a culture of keeping our books well and stayed on the right side of the law.

Perhaps what may have turned out to be for the benefit of ABC Transport, was my tendency to be detailed, to keep proper books and be organised. These traits came because of my father's influence. When I was in secondary school, he used to make me account for all the books I had. He forced me to have a register where I documented all my books, especially those that I used in school. My father would check this register frequently and get me to account for the books on a regular basis. I think it gave me a sense of accountability so when I got into business, accountability became important to me, right from the start. Anyone who worked with me also had to be accountable. I remember those early days when I would go to a petrol station to buy petrol and request for receipts after buying. The petrol attendants were only used to company car drivers requesting for receipts, so they were always taken aback by this young man asking them for receipts after buying petrol. Some of them would ask, "Are you from a company? Why are you asking for receipts?" I never used to move until they gave me receipts. People on the queue would complain bitterly and ask me to move out of the line but I would act deaf. I felt I needed to account for every money spent.

As I grew in business, I knew this trait was a big asset in our attempt to build a good brand. We wanted a company that would be strong and reputable. It became clear to me that if you don't do things right, you are not going to be turn out well. I made sure that we kept proper books and we focused on adding value rather than chasing money. The effort we put into Coach West Africa for instance, could have been put into other profitable areas of our business but we would have missed the chance to be impactful. No one can take away our role in history when it comes to opening the West African Coast for tourism and commerce. This is what our efforts achieved

IN 1998 THERE MAY BE NO LUXURY

BUSES IN NIGERIA

YES! Because the cost of purchase and running your favourite long-distance buses may be beyond the reach of every transporter.

	1993	1995
Cost of luxury bus	N4 million	N16 million
Import duty	5%	25%
Cost of 12.00 tire	N16,000	N33,000
Cost of brake lining (set)	N3,000	N17,000
Average rate of change of tire	2 tires	5 tires
Bank interest rate on lease	21%	47%
Condition of Highways	Fair	Inaccessible
Average trips per week	6	4

Already many transporters have withdrawn 50% of their fleet from the roads.

Dear customer, support your transporter in these times of frustration by showing understanding.

Effective 6th October, 1995, our new fare shall be N850.00

ABC Transport

- *Corruption hurt the road transport industry in Nigeria in many ways. We were forced to increase our rates a few times due to deteriorating economic circumstances. The above is a sample notification we published when forced to increase our rates.*

Integrity is a requirement for
building a strong, durable brand.

Decide early on your ethical and
moral standards in business.

Be detailed. Keep your
books tidy. You never know
who will check tomorrow.

Pragmatism is an essential trait for
succeeding in business in Nigeria.

A good reputation opens doors,
attracts businesses, brings helpful
partnerships and secures the loyalty
of talented employees.

PART III

GOING BEYOND BOUNDARIES

CHAPTER EIGHT

Breaking Into the West Coast
"Often in Business, If You Don't Expand, You Die"

When you are into business or any kind of venture, you must constantly think about how to grow, expand and reach new horizons. Those who succeed in business never sit still. They are always innovating and creating new products and services. Your phone is a typical example. No matter the brand you use, you will hear of an updated version of your phone every year. As it is with Apple, so it is with Samsung, Nokia and the rest of the popular phone makers. Success should always be a motivating factor for doing more, not a reason for doing less. You must always dream big and always desire your business to break into new grounds. For business people in Nigeria, this, at times, could mean looking beyond the shores of your country. We have indeed reached a stage when we must be thinking about expanding our businesses overseas first of all because the opportunities are limitless once you start thinking along that line but also because it is a way of earning foreign exchange for Nigeria and improving the country's international image.

Expanding your thinking in this regard requires faith. You need to believe in the possibilities out there and never look down on yourself as someone who can only play locally. The world has changed. It is a global village we live in now. The opportunities that exist are tremendous and technology has made it a lot easier to take advantage of those opportunities, but it is only those who think far and big that can realize these.

After we had done business in the road transport sector for about eleven years, I began to think about new ways we could take ABC Transport to another level and add more value to our customers and industry. I thought that one of the ways to do that was by offering more premium services, so I began to think about the West African Coast. Along that coast is Nigeria, Benin Republic, Togo, Ghana, Cote D'Ivoire, Liberia, Sierra Leone, Guinea, Guinea Bissau, The Gambia and

Senegal. Add the countries that are not 'coastal' and you will have a total of eighteen countries. Admittedly, a region that has experienced the Nigerian Civil War, the Liberian Civil Wars, the Guinea-Bissau Civil War, Ivorian Civil War and the Sierra Leone Rebel War within a single generation, has to be described as troubled. Nevertheless, it is a region with much untapped potential. The vast natural resources, massive population of over 362 million people and the Atlantic Ocean lining the western boundary of the region, present immense opportunities for the area.

At the time I began to seriously consider the West Africa idea, Ghana was the attraction among the coastal countries because the country had gradually become the star of the region in terms of political stability, development, economic growth and tourism. Sites like the Kwame Nkrumah Mausoleum, Kakum National Park, the Mole National Park, Cape Coast Castle, Elmina Castle, Nzulezo and Osu Castle had began playing host to many tourists from around the world and more people from countries like Nigeria had started seeing them as places they could visit on holiday trips.

Unfortunately, due to a few bad diplomatic experiences in the past, Ghanaians were no longer visiting Nigeria as they used to do and vice versa. The story is captured in the famous expression 'Ghana Must Go' which has its origin in a pronouncement made by Alhaji Shehu Shagari, Nigeria's former President, in 1983. Shagari held a press conference in which he ordered all immigrants in Nigeria without the right papers to leave the country within a few weeks. "If they don't leave, they should be arrested and tried, and sent back to their homes. Illegal immigrants under normal circumstances, should not be given any notice whatsoever. If you break a law, then you have to pay for it", Shagari had reportedly said.

It is claimed by Nigerian officials that the pronouncement affected one million Ghanaians and another million from the other West African countries. The oil boom of the 1970s in Nigeria, had attracted most of them. I am not sure Shagari expected the international community's outrage that followed his pronouncement. He was criticized by human right activists, diplomats and foreign governments. Over two million people including the Ghanaians put what they had in what became known as 'Ghana Must Go' bags, a large stripped bag characterised by its chequered appearance which became the symbol of the exodus.

Most of those who fled Nigeria, went through the Seme Border into Benin Republic where they could find a ship to cross to Ghana. Jerry Rawlings, the military head of state of Ghana at the time, had closed the road borders between Ghana and Togo and to avoid a refugee crisis on its hands, Togo in turn had closed its borders with Benin Republic. Rawlings and the then Togolese leader, Gnassingbé Eyadéma, eventually opened the road borders for the refugees to cross.

That experience worsened the Nigeria – Ghana relations which had previously been strained earlier in the late sixties when Ghana asked Nigerians and other illegal immigrants to leave its shores. Like Shagari's pronouncements some years later, Ghana's expulsion of foreigners had stirred up controversies and bad blood.

It was against that background that we started our push towards our Coach West Africa initiative. Although the relationship between Nigeria and Ghana had improved since the 'Ghana Must Go' saga, the border situations had stifled what could potentially have been a much more vibrant relationship between the two countries. But since their exodus from Nigeria, Ghanaians had picked themselves up and built their country into an enviable one in West Africa. The country was opening and beginning to bask in the reputation of being the best place to visit in the West Africa region.

At the time I began to think about West Africa, I also noticed that middle class Nigerians were big on travelling but they did so mainly to Europe and America. "What if we could make going to Ghana, easy and comfortable by road? We can break into the West Coast. We can be the first company to do that", I thought. But road trips across the West African Coast was not easy at all and there was no road company in the business of taking people across the coast in an organized and formal manner back then. Crossing the borders used to be horrific. To get to Ghana from Nigeria, you needed to cross six borders – out of Nigeria, into Benin Republic, out of Benin Republic, into Togo, out of Togo, into Ghana – and each experience was difficult for travellers. People had to wait for very long periods for their vehicles to be cleared at each border before they moved on.

I began to research. First, I sent a gentleman, Alban Igwe, who was doing an intern programme with ABC Transport, to travel by road across West Africa up to Ivory Coast and return with a survey report. He went and returned after a week with a 'findings document'. We looked at his report and saw all the bottlenecks we needed to deal with. The challenges looked daunting. New ideas are often like that, giving you many reasons why you should dump them and stick to what you are used to. But the report also proved that there was an opportunity to be explored. We got thinking about all the possible business options we could take in that situation. "Were we going to be just a transport company, or should we explore tourism?" we pondered. Eventually, we settled for the latter since tourism was an FX earner and would be more exciting for customers and the countries involved.

While thinking about the option preferred, I decided I needed to share my researcher's experience so one Sunday morning, I took off to Ghana with a friend of mine called Steve and a driver. We started the journey from Ikeja, Lagos and headed to Accra, Ghana. We went through all the borders and experienced the challenges other travellers experienced. While going, I was on the lookout for any transport company travelling that route but found none until we got in between Togo and Accra. We saw a bus labelled PERGAH Transport that had a tire problem. We stopped and approached the bus. The driver was a friendly man who explained the problem he was having. So, we helped and while doing that, I engaged the man to find out what his company was into. He said it was a Ghanaian company and they were on charter to Togo. It turned out to be an informative conversation. When we returned to Nigeria, I contacted an old friend, Mr. Bainey who was Ghanaian. We had done some business in the past when Rapido Ventures was supplying audio visual equipment and he had been one of our customers then.

I asked Mr. Bainey if he could help me get some contacts in Ghana we could collaborate with when we were set to start the tourism trips. He obliged and got us some good contacts. Coincidentally, one of the contacts he brought was the managing director of PERGAH Transport. Interestingly, by the time we were set to start, we appointed PERGAH Transport as our handling agent in Ghana since we had no office or staff over there.

Those preliminary moves were all well and good but clearly, the key was the Economic Community of West African States (ECOWAS). There was no way we were going to make a success of the West Coast trips unless things improved at the borders and for that to happen, ECOWAS needed to step in. So off I went to the ECOWAS Secretariat in Abuja to make a presentation. It was about the opportunities ECOWAS States were losing to the border situations that made travels difficult. I told ECOWAS that West Africa was missing a lot by not opening up the borders and making road travels easy for the different citizens of the neighbouring states. They were impressed with my presentation and apparently, they had also been concerned about the situation. It was so bad that at times to get things from Ghana to Nigeria speedily, they had to first take them through London by air and then from London to Nigeria. The same thing happened when they needed to move things from Nigeria to Ghana. Courier companies preferred that London route to travelling directly to each country.

Perhaps the biggest problem we both agreed on was the ignorance of the various immigration officers. Most of them were not even aware of what their responsibilities to neighbouring countries were and they resorted to taking tips. Travellers too did not know their rights, so they succumbed easily to harassments and blackmails by immigration officers.

We explained all these observations to the ECOWAS officials and told them that our plan was to simply package tourism offers for travellers and ensure we could get them from Nigeria to different West African countries and back. They were really interested and wanted to know what we needed. I asked them to do us a letter for the ministries of tourism in Nigeria, Benin Republic, Togo and Ghana. They did the letters and I went to have them delivered. That triggered a series of events that led to the birth of our Coach West Africa adventure. It was to change the course of ABC Transport and the lives of many West Africans.

One thing that is important for me to point out here is that whenever you decide to expand your horizon you must also be committed to studying hard and researching on your new idea. When you do this, you make a lot of discoveries and you will begin to realize there are many things simply waiting to be explored. A relevant example here is when I stumbled upon the ECOWAS Treaty, a multilateral agreement signed by the member states of ECOWAS. The Treaty was meant to make West Africa like a mega country. I realized that the Treaty provided for easy travels across West African borders, that all you needed to travel easily across the borders was an

ECOWAS Travel Certificate or an ID card showing you are a citizen of an ECOWAS State. The discovery blew my mind. I was excited at the possibilities West Africans had if only they knew about the Treaty.

Another example is my discovery of what is called the ECOWAS Trade Liberalization Scheme (ETLS) which permits local manufacturers to take products from one West African State to another without paying duties. Many people did not know this and other opportunities. I decided it was time to become an advocate of that Treaty.

THE ECOWAS TREATY

"The Economic Community of West African States (ECOWAS) Treaty is a multilateral agreement signed by the member states that made up the Economic Community of West African States. The initial treaty was signed by the Heads of States and Governments of the then 16 member states in 1975 in Lagos, Nigeria. With new developments and mandates for the Community a revised treaty was signed in Cotonou, Benin Republic in July, 1993 by the heads of states and government of the now 15 member states.

The signing of the revised treaty further bound the sovereign states into agreeing on 93 different Articles, which they have agreed to work together as a single regional economic block. By signing the revised treaty member states reaffirmed the Treaty establishing the Economic Community of West African States signed in Lagos on 28 May, 1975 and considered its achievements.

The member states were conscious of the over-riding need to encourage, foster and accelerate the economic and social development of member States in order to improve the living standards of the peoples. Therefore, the Heads of States and Governments were convinced that the promotion of harmonious economic development of the States called for effective economic co-operation and integration largely through a determined and concerted policy of self-reliance

They took into consideration the African Charter on Human and People's Rights and the Declaration of Political Principles of the Economic Community of West African States adopted in Abuja by the Fourteenth Ordinary Session of the Authority of Heads of State and Government on 6 July, 1991 and were further convinced that the integration of the Member States into a viable regional Community may demand the partial and gradual pooling of national sovereignties to the Community within the context of a collective political will.

They therefore accepted the need to establish Community Institutions vested with relevant and adequate powers, noting that the present bilateral and multilateral forms of economic co-operation within the region open up perspectives for more extensive co-operation.

The Heads of States and Government on behalf of their

countries accepted the need to face together the political, economic and socio-cultural challenges of the present and the future, and to pool together the resources of their peoples while respecting their diversities for the most rapid and optimum expansion of the region's productive capacity.

They further took into consideration the Lagos Plan of Action and the Final Act of Lagos of April 1980 stipulating the establishment, by the year 2000, of an African Economic Community based on existing and future regional economic communities and was mindful of the Treaty establishing the African Economic Community signed in Abuja on 3 June, 1991.

They then affirmed that the final goal is the accelerated and sustained economic development of Member States, culminating in the economic union of West Africa....."

Economic Community of West African State

(ECOWAS)

On the day we commissioned the project, we put up a bit of fanfare. We travelled with representatives of Nigeria Tourism Development Corporation (NTDC) including their director general, Mrs. Omotayo Omotosho. Before then, we had approached NTDC and given them a presentation on what we were planning to do. They had been impressed and keen on seeing how we would execute our plans. That first trip turned out to be an eye opener for Mrs. Omotayo Omotosho and her team. They could see what Nigerians were missing and all that Ghana had done to improve its tourism initiatives. The next day, we had a ceremony in Accra with the Ghanaian Tourism Board. It provided the NTDC the opportunity to see the things being done by the Ghanaian Government.

The CAN investment that came in 2003 was what helped us to kick start the West Coast trips in 2004. The money brought in aided us in buying buses for the routes and complete the building of the Amuwo Odofin Terminal which we referred to as the West Coast Terminal. We tried to model that terminal after airports. We got officers of the National Drug Law Enforcement Agency (NDLEA) there so that instead of travellers getting their bags opened and checked at each border, the NDLEA officers at the terminal did all the searches, sealed the bags and put tags on them. With that, travellers could move across the boarders without anyone opening their bags. We still have the NDLEA officers at that terminal today.

Overall, the West Coast travels and tourism project served as a platform for us to boost tourism in West Africa, change the way Nigeria was being perceived, open the Nigeria – Ghana trade route, take the ABC brand to a whole new level and earn us more money than the trips we were making between Lagos and Abuja did. It was so successful that there was a period we were doing fifteen trips a day during Christmas season. Our strategy was to target tourists rather than traders or business people. That was why we got a tour operator in Ghana who could take travellers around Ghana. We packaged different types of tours with different rates. We had two-day tours, three-day tours, one-week tours, Valentine tours and so on. We broke the barriers between Nigeria and Ghana. Coach West Africa reopened Nigeria to Ghana after the 'Ghana Must Go' saga. Families began to travel between Nigeria and Ghana more often. After we opened the route, other transport companies began to explore it.

There were also some other side benefits of venturing into the West Coast. It was while at the ECOWAS Secretariat that someone first mentioned Nigerian Export - Import Bank (NEXIM) to me. He said, "Mr. Nneji, have you ever heard of NEXIM Bank?"

I said, "What's NEXIM Bank?"

He explained, "Nigerian Export-Import Bank. It is an export credit agency in Nigeria, established by the Federal Government of Nigeria to replace the Nigerian Export Credit Guarantee & Insurance Corporation. It provides export credit guarantees and export credit insurance for exports of Nigerian commodities and services within and outside West Africa."

"Interesting. I am just learning about it for the first time." I responded, genuinely fascinated.

"NEXIM provides export credit guarantee, credit in local currency and manages funds connected with exports. It also maintains foreign exchange revolving fund for lending to exporters who need to import foreign inputs to facilitate export production. What I think you will find most interesting is that NEXIM currently provides short and medium term loans to Nigerian exporters", he explained further.

I was visibly stunned. How could there be such an opportunity and I never knew about it? Somehow, throughout my researching period, NEXIM Bank never crossed my radar.

"If you succeed with your plan to move people across West Africa, you could get financing from them at single digit interest rates because what you are planning to do is classified as exporting. You will be earning foreign exchange for the country", he concluded.

I was excited and immediately began to plan how to leverage on NEXIM. When we started the Nigeria-Ghana trips, I went straight to the bank and they gave ABC Transport loans at single digit interest rates, just like I had been told. That was a time when some of our competitors were getting loans at 25 – 30% interest rates. For a long time after that first contact, we kept our relationship with NEXIM Bank active based on the West Coast of Africa business. Our relationship with the bank grew over the years and at a point in time, we became one of their best customers. We even received an award from them.

You can see from my narratives in this chapter that venturing into the West African Coast, was major in ABC Transport's history and it all started with a desire to find more premium values for customers and explore new territories. You have also seen that like any other idea, project or pursuit, it came with its own big challenges. Perhaps the biggest of the challenges in that whole process of starting the Coach West Africa project was trying to formalize a business or system that had been operating for a long time in an informal and somewhat chaotic way. Before we got into the business, people were travelling between Nigeria and Ghana but the problem was that the existing travelling system was not properly structured, was reeked in ignorance and corruption and was always uncomfortable for most travellers. It was difficult attempting to change things. After we started, we had to occasionally go back to the tourism boards of Benin Republic and Togo to complain to them about happenings at their borders because at times their men did not understand the right things to do. There was also the language barrier because Togo and Benin Republic are Francophone countries while Nigeria and Ghana are Anglophone countries. Anyone doing business across those countries knows that language can be a challenge. The way we solved the problem was to hire bilingual crews. We hired cabin executives who could speak both French and English.

Another important lesson here is that you need to be able to leverage on existing resources and structures. We leveraged on ECOWAS, NTDC and partners in Ghana. We didn't need to start renting or buying houses in Ghana. We relied on existing operators over there and we did that for about four years before incorporating ABC Ghana Limited because we had grown and our partners didn't have the capacity to handle the cargo component of our business.

As an entrepreneur, you must expand your horizon. You must think big. If you are in transportation, think tourism because transportation is a critical element of tourism. You have to look at opportunities along the entire value chain. We have come a long way in our Coach West Africa adventure. I am glad that Ghana appreciates our efforts. Over the years, each time there is a tourism event in the country, ABC Transport is acknowledged. We have been given awards in Ghana several times and I have been recognized as one of the top personalities in tourism in West Africa and 2015, I was voted as the personality of the year in tourism by Travel Magazine, an African Tourism publication. I am not mentioning these awards to flaunt them. I do so with a deep sense of gratitude for how much ABC Transport has been able to achieve through the Coach West Africa effort. It is amazing how ordinary ideas can turn into significant things if we only believe and apply ourselves.

Think about growing.

Be passionate about growing.

Dream about growing.

Break out of your mould.
There are always new horizons
in business. Don't' get stuck in
one spot for too long.

Think leverage.
There are always partnerships
that can help to make your
dream happen.

In exploring new opportunities,
there are always things to learn.

Two of ABC Transport buses that travel along the West African Coast.

CHAPTER NINE

——◆◆◆——

Keep Expanding

*"Continuously looking for ways to add value to customers
can help you create multiple streams of income"*

I used the story of how we expanded into the West African Coast to illustrate how a business can grow when you keep focusing on adding value to customers and your industry, exploring the entire value chain of a business and generally stretching your boundaries. These are extremely important points to emphasize. If you want to succeed in business, you must create multiple streams of income and to create multiple streams of income you have to constantly look for how you can add value to your customers and to do that, you have to always explore the entire value chain of your business. Exploring the entire value chain of our own business meant we had to look beyond being a bus company to being a transportation company and once we started thinking transportation, we naturally started thinking logistics. The moment we began to think about transportation beyond the shores of Nigeria, we naturally began to think about tourism. That's how it works. You must look beyond the immediate thing you are doing and ask yourself what more you can do to better serve customers. Are there add on services and products you can offer? Are there new partners you can take on to expand? Is there something else your customers want that you can provide but you are not providing now? Can your business lead to a related one? These are questions you must ask regularly and find answers to. A business often has endless possibilities yet it is often unexplored by its owner.

It is in line with this that after we had been in the transportation business for a while, I started to feel it was necessary to create support services. One of the ideas we came up with was what we called Transit Support Services Limited (TSSL) to provide ancillary services like importation of tires and other vehicle parts, fabrication of car parts, provision of fibre glass materials and local manufacturing of small components for the road transport industry. This subsidiary company became a reliable service provider for efficient fleet operations.

In 2013 / 2014, an automotive policy for Nigeria was launched by the Federal Government and companies were asked to leverage on it to start local assembling and manufacturing of vehicles. I felt we could take advantage of this auto policy because of our experience in the road transport sector and also because, as a consequence, we had a lot of automobile engineers and mechanics who could provide us with a manpower base if we wanted to go into local assembling and manufacturing of vehicles. For over twenty years, these technicians had fixed our vehicles and had mastered everything needed to keep our buses running well. I felt we were knowledgeable enough to take the vehicles apart and assemble them.

So, we applied for the assembly license using Transit Support Services Limited as the business carrier and fortunately, the government granted us the license. I am not sure about the number of other companies the government granted licenses to when we got ours, but I know there are about twenty to thirty companies with similar licences in Nigeria today even though the active ones among them are less than ten.

Getting that license when we did, marked a new beginning for us. It was an exciting new industry to explore but we knew that to go far with the project we needed to acquire franchises and establish partnerships because motor assembling is a very capital-intensive industry.

After we received the licence, we approached Anambra Auto Manufacturing Company (ANAMMCO) which at that point had been shut down for about seven years. The Federal Government of Nigeria had built ANAMMCO in partnership with Mercedes for local production of commercial vehicles in the 1980s. It was one of the five auto assembly plants in Nigeria with the others being Peugeot, Volkswagen, Styr and Leyland. That was during the golden era of local manufacturing. The plants were massive investments with hundreds of hectares each. Unfortunately, the ANAMMCO project died just as Peugeot, Volkswagen and others did during the years of socio-economic downturns in Nigeria. The Federal Government then decided to privatize ANAMMCO and sold its shares in that regard. We went to them with the proposal to use the facility to produce trucks and get back some of their workers who had left them. By then, the core investor had become Chief G.U. Okeke. It was him we approached for a partnership. ANAMMCO agreed to enter a partnership with us in which they would lease the manufacturing facility to us.

That was done under a manufacturing agreement we signed in 2014. We also brought in Shaanxi Heavy Duty Automobiles (SHDA) of China, which was the manufacturer of Shacman in China, as partners.

Prior to then, we had been using Shacman Trucks in Nigeria and I might even say that we made the brand popular not only by using it but by also offering it to the market. When the auto policy came out, we thought we could start assembling locally, what we had been importing from China. So, I introduced the auto policy to SHDA and told the Chinese they could make money here in Nigeria if they partnered with us to assemble trucks locally. One day, the Chinese company called to invite me over to China for a presentation and meeting. It was a very cold January morning when I delivered that presentation in China. I made the presentation to their board. I told them about how duties were robbing them of business expansion and consequently, profits in Nigeria. I told them that with the auto policy, they could join us to assemble locally and therefore make the trucks cheaper in Nigeria. That way, the brand could become popular and they could then make more money because of that. They were obviously impressed. The next month, they sent a delegation to Nigeria and I took them to ANAMMCO for assessment of the facility. We signed an agreement and started bringing in the components.

With Shaanxi's partnership, we took off and started assembling vehicles, with a capacity to build fifty trucks every week. Our partnerships turned out to be very successful and in 2017, we assembled about one thousand trucks in Nigeria with Dangote Group being our major customer. We now have 200 Nigerians and nineteen expatriates working for us in the business. The expatriates have been beneficial in providing technical and quality control. They have also provided training and technology transfer to us.

I will be the first to admit that local assembling and manufacturing of vehicles is not exactly an easy business to veer into. Right now, many vehicle manufacturers would love to come to Nigeria to assemble their vehicles but because of poor infrastructure, lack of power and other socioeconomic problems, they stay away. Another thing that hinders production in Nigeria is the absence of proper vehicle finance schemes as it is South Africa, the USA and other countries where you don't have to pay cash in full to buy a vehicle.

But the challenges notwithstanding, I believe you must do what you must do. We forged on despite the difficulties. We went ahead with local manufacturing and provision of maintenance services for our trucks. We had to be well equipped with the after sales services. We leveraged on our knowledge of the industry for this. For example, we provide support services for over 1,000 trucks for Dangote Group.

This is an example of how to explore different aspects of a business. Sometimes you have a business with redundant resources. Your job is to seek for ways to turn those redundant resources into useful ones. We did not need to hire another chief engineer when we started assembling because we already had one. We leveraged on our internal administrative structures and systems. We moved personnel around. We used what we already had, added partnerships and opened a new but related line of business.

We stumbled on a business because we were trying to find different ways of adding value and we were seeking for how we could exploit the entire value chain of our business. This is how to make money. Think about the entire value chain in whatever industry you are operating in.

Abex Parcel Services

Another example that is relevant to my advice on exploring your entire value chain when seeking to add more value to your customers is Abex Parcel Services which we started as an offshoot of ABC Transport's experiences in parcel and cash transfer services. As we grew, we realized that more people were asking our drivers to help them drop things and money for loved ones at the destinations. This got us thinking about charging customers for this service and so we started doing so. As time passed, it became almost natural for us to begin to think of a courier business. This idea became a reality in 1997 when we established Abex Parcel Services. 40% of the new company's issued share capital of 16.5 million was owned by ABC Transport while the remaining shares were owned by five other close friends with the next largest single shareholding being 25%.

I think the timing for Abex was inspired. The courier business in Nigeria grew fast from the mid-eighties because of the decline of NIPOST. By 1997, more than 43 companies had emerged in the courier service industry. The increase in the number of operators brought about rapid development of the industry in terms of new products and improved services. The total industry revenue in 1996 was about 800 million naira and the annual growth rate was about 3%. The market leaders were all multi-nationals and had access to the facilities of their overseas parents. UPS, DHL and TNT and FedEx were all linked to the global network of their parent companies. This enabled them to track documents while on transit anywhere in the world and to obtain proof of delivery immediately it occurred. The main strategy Abex adopted was to solve the problem of high prices of parcel delivery services by offering them at lower rates than the existing courier companies. We planned to charge N600 for the first 5kg whereas the average rate for other courier companies was N700 for the first 0.5kg and N800 for the next 1kg.

Abex turned out well and like ABC Transport, despite existing competitors, we simply found niches we could operate in to provide problem solving services to our customers. This is the way to think in business. The possibilities before you are endless. You just need to have a passion for finding and adding value to customers and your industry. That passion is what will drive you to explore opportunities.

To succeed in business,
you need to create multiple
streams of income.

To create multiple streams
of income, you have to explore
the entire value chain of
your business.

To explore the entire value
chain of your business,
you need to be looking for
values you can add to your
customers & industry.

Trucks assembled at ANAMMCO

At Abex Lawn Tennis Tournament, Ikeja Club, 2006

With guests at Shacman Assembly flag off, ANAMMCO, 2015

Welcoming guests at Shacman Assembly flag off at ANAMMCO, 2015

CHAPTER TEN

—·—◄◙◙◙►·—

Beyond Profits

*"Get involved in advocacy. If you don't fix the problems that
plague your society, they will come back to haunt you"*

As an entrepreneur or business owner, it is important to always remember that your responsibility goes beyond building your business or brand. You must also focus on contributing to the general wellbeing of your profession, industry and society. The reason for this is straightforward: we all operate within contexts. Nobody functions in isolation. If there are problems in your environment, they will affect you. A business person has a responsibility to his or her society. This is why I have always been involved in advocacy efforts in the road transport sector in Nigeria.

When I came up with the idea of ABC Transport, two words stood out for me as the most descriptive of what I had in mind for the business: 'Safety' and 'Comfort'. The safety aspect of this was very crucial because the era ABC Transport started was when road accidents became most pronounced in Nigeria. There was a bus brand then called J-5 that was popularly used for cross city road transportation in the country back then. Many accidents involved this bus and it was apparent to a lot of people that for whatever reasons, it was accident prone. When ABC Transport started, I was determined to assure people they could feel safe in our buses. I decided it was important to train our drivers properly and part of that was getting the Federal Road Safety Commission (FRSC) involved in our training programmes. So, we did exactly that and it triggered a long-term relationship between ABC Transport and FRSC. The Sector Commander of FRSC, Owerri, Tesma Regha, after he retired, ended up joining us at ABC Transport and he is still with us today as our head of safety.

FRSC trained our drivers to understand basic safety requirement and skills for drivers so much so that we became confident that passengers in our buses were guaranteed safety whenever they travelled with us. As our rapport with

FRSC improved, I realized that safety was not just about ABC Transport, it was something every bus company needed to take seriously, and something Nigeria needed to give top priority. It became imperative that I had to take the subject of safety to our entire industry. In line with that, we established what we called, 'Safety Week' every December. It grew to be a major event where the FRSC, National Union of Road Transport Workers (NURTW), other competing companies, expert lecturers and members of the public shared experiences and rubbed minds together.

At a point, the FRSC noticed we were prominent in road safety advocacy so they turned to us for resource persons whenever they had major events around the country. I used every opportunity we were given to propose ideas on the best ways to keep our roads safe. Part of what we pushed for is what is called Road Transport Safety Standardization Scheme.

Part of the objective of the scheme was to ensure that every organisation – private or public - with up to five vehicles in their fleet, becomes classified as a 'Fleet Operator', appoints a safety officer and complies with the FRSC requirements on certification, registration and safety officers to build a data bank for ease of monitoring and to ensure better and safer road usage. I was very much involved in making this happen.

Also, we realized that one of the major causes of accidents in Nigeria, was over speeding and so we started thinking seriously about how we could help to curb it. We tried different things. First, we decided to be monitoring departure and arrival times of our drivers and used that to get a sense of what they were doing and how fast they were travelling.

We also established a system we tagged, 'The Passengers Watch Card' or POWA Cards in our vehicles, which empowered passengers to monitor and report drivers who drove recklessly through special numbers they could call. As technology progressed, we were the first operators to have the speed limiters in our vehicles. We carried that same 'Safe Speed' advocacy to the Federal Road Safety Corps, telling them that Speed Limiters needed to be enforced.

I was a member of the technical committee on 'Speed Limiters' along with the Nigeria Society of Engineers and the Federal Road Safety Corps. Using experiences ABC Transport had gathered, I demonstrated to the committee, how we had been able to reduce accidents using speed limiting devices.

Fortunately, they bought into it and eventually the bill for speed limiters was passed in the House of Assembly. Going to the National Assembly to explain and defend that bill a few times before it was passed, is one of my fondest memories. I am not sure if anything beats the feeling you have knowing that what you are fighting for can save many lives.

Apart from safe driving, I also got involved in advocating for better roads in Nigeria. I was partly instrumental in setting up the Federal Road Maintenance Agency (FERMA) which was Nigeria's first institutional mechanism for monitoring and maintaining all Federal roads in the country. My involvement started with a burden of concern I had earlier. I was so worried about the state of our roads that in 2002, I invited some journalists to take a bus ride with us from Lagos to some other parts of Nigeria, make observations and return to their news organisations to report their experiences and observations. We lodged the journalists in hotels and drove them around for them to see for themselves what our drivers saw every day. It was an eye opening experience for the journalists. As agreed, when they returned, they reported their experiences and that created some buzz in the country. But I felt the impact wasn't as much as I wanted. Therefore,

I called a guy named Iyk Ekeoma who managed a company called Nectar Production which had been working with ABC Transport in the production of video entertainment content used in the buses. I got him to make a 10-day road trip around Nigeria along with our operational personnel and capture his observations in video. He did exactly that and handed over a twenty minutes documentary titled, 'Our Road: A Treacherous Journey'. The documentary summed up how bad Nigerian roads had become.

Watching that documentary was moving for me. It reminded me of what I had always realized as a road transporter in Nigeria: that we had a poor maintenance culture. Our road development trajectory had never aligned with our economic development trajectory. We moved too many things by road because we failed to build a railway system. We had also failed to develop a safety culture to the extent that even if the roads got better, there was no guarantee they would become safer. There were accidents that occurred because the roads were bad but more accidents happened because people over sped and generally had bad driving habits. Many were overtaking from the right side of the roads. When we talk about safer roads, it doesn't mean roads without potholes, but a number of things ranging from adherence to the use of road markings and speed limits and other things like respect for fellow road users. When I got involved in advocacy for road safety, things were really bad in Nigeria not just in terms of actual road quality but in terms of the driving culture most Nigerians had.

I felt that a major problem was a disconnection between Nigerian leaders and our roads. Most of them flew from city to city so they had no idea how bad the roads had become. Well, that was about to change, at least to a reasonable extent. I somehow got the then minister of works, Chief Tony Anenih to watch the documentary we had created and encouraged him to get President Olusegun Obasanjo to also watch it. They both did and things moved quickly after then. A meeting was summoned and a Road Maintenance Task Force was set up. I was invited to be a member of that task force as a representative of the road transport industry. The task force was responsible for emergency repairs among other things. The primary concerns of the government were the problems our documentary highlighted. The government wanted them fixed immediately. It was while I was serving as a member of the task force that the FERMA bill was drafted. I was involved in developing that bill and I was a pioneer member of the FERMA Board of Directors.

Part of what we also did was to review the state of toll gates around Nigeria. We wanted to get the toll gates to generate more income and channel the money made to road maintenance. But surprisingly, President Obasanjo suddenly demolished the toll gates for reasons best known to him.

One observation I made during that experience was that many Nigerian professionals only complain a lot about Nigeria. Very few get involved in fixing things. Everybody is focused on doing their own things and very few try to find solutions at the societal or industry levels. But this is unwise. People need to rise up and try to protect their enterprises because the government's action or inaction affects every business.

Many of the things we ignore at the societal levels return to haunt us in our businesses. For us in our industry, because for a long time we had all showed little interest in advocacy, all the roads had nearly collapsed. For example, it had become almost impossible to travel to Owerri without going through bush paths. Of course, I know that engaging the public sector in Nigeria at any level can be difficult. For instance, people were insinuating that I had an agenda. They thought I was pushing for things for myself. They didn't believe I genuinely wanted to make contributions to my industry and country. They didn't know that getting involved in such advocacy cost me a lot of personal resources. I spent nights working on policies; I spent my money researching and organising and I spent a lot of time making presentations and giving speeches in different places.

But these challenges must never deter us from getting involved and doing our best to improve things. Till today, one of the most satisfying feelings comes from knowing that my contributions in that Task Force made a difference. It was the Task Force that repaired the Onitsha - Owerri Road which is part of the trans-national high way. Apart from that road, the Task Force pressured the government to place high priority on other important Federal highways. I saw roads fixed. I saw important laws enacted. I saw safety measures implemented. I saw FERMA birthed. I saw and experienced a lot of things that made a difference in Nigeria's road transport sector.

So, it is important to appreciate the fact that growing a business successfully also places on the entrepreneur or business owner, the responsibility to get involved in improving his or her industry, society and country. Like I have said throughout this book, it's not primarily about making money but about adding value. When you approach business with this paradigm, you will likely reap incredible benefits from your efforts.

Always look beyond
your own business.

Always think about how to
improve your industry.

Always remember that your business
needs the right 'industry environment'
to truly succeed.

To be outstanding in business,
you must make outstanding
contributions to your industry.

When you are involved in advocacy
efforts in your industry, you are doing
yourself and your business a favour.

PART IV

BUSINESS REALITIES

CHAPTER ELEVEN

Realities of Business

"Are there really 'keys to business success'?"

As you would have noticed in this book, I believe there are numerous factors that come into play for different people as far as succeeding in business is concerned and I have been around long enough to know that there is really nothing like, 'The Five Secrets to Business Success'. Whoever says, "These are the only five things you need to succeed in business", is either naïve or mischievous. However, it is true that to succeed in business and indeed in any area of endeavour, there are universal principles or laws that are important to apply. Whether it is hard work, persistence or focus, most of us already know that unless we implement certain principles, we will likely fail in whatever it is we are doing. In this book, I have already outlined a few things I consider to be important when it comes to starting or building a business but here, I want to explore a few others that caught my attention as I started and grew in business. If any young person were to ask me to offer tips on what to look out for as one embarks on any business journey, here are a few of the things I would consider to be vital.

1. Vision Is Essential

I believe every young entrepreneur needs to have a vision of what he wants his business to become. Some people will say you must see every detail of what is ahead before you can achieve it. I'm not sure about that and I don't think that's how it works in real life. But I do agree that you will need to have a broad picture of what you want to build. As a young entrepreneur, I had a desire to run a big organization. I didn't have a specific size in mind but I wanted an organization that would be national in outlook and touch every nook and cranny of Nigeria. Today, I am glad that ABC Transport conducts businesses across the country and beyond.

My thinking back then was that the bigger your company is, the more lives you can touch, the more impact you can make, and the more satisfaction you can get. It was just a desire I had, a vision of the future I kept in my heart. Some people prefer business models that keep them small while they make a lot of money. That's fine but that's not me. You need to be yourself and do what fits for you.

My thinking then and now is that there's a difference between how much money you earn and how much impact you make. You can make a lot of impact without making as much money and you can make a lot of money without making as much impact. You just have to figure out what your preference is. But whether you want to build a big business or not, it's essential to have a broad vision of what you want to aspire to.

Like I said earlier, I have always been driven by the desire to create value than to make money. When you want to create value, it often means you want to make an impact. The transport business is not as lucrative as some will have you believe. It's a difficult business with small profit margins for many reasons. For example, tax laws are not developed well enough for service-based businesses in Nigeria. In the transport sector, you don't get most of the kinds of tax relief concessions manufacturing companies get. Even companies like Greyhound in the USA, don't make as much money as some think so the reality of small profit margins in the sector, is global. Someone might think that because we have the advantage of 'volume' in the road transport sector, we should be making a lot of money but that's just not the reality. Over the years, ABC Transport has expanded into cargo logistics, haulage and a few other services. It is interesting to realize that the aspect of our business that makes the least money for us, is our passenger operations which, ironically, is the one that makes the most impact nationally. More people know about our passenger operations than any other aspect of our business. People look at its revenue but forget that revenue is different from profit. However, I am excited by the fact that all over Nigeria and West Africa, people think about ABC Transport when considering travelling by road. It fits in well with the broad vision I had as a young entrepreneur.

I believe this is important for anyone starting out in business. Rarely do people succeed when they do not clarify what they want.

2. Competition Is Fierce and It Is Never Fair

You will get into trouble if you don't embrace the reality that competition exists and is often fierce in every market. Perhaps more significantly, competition is hardly ever fair. Many times you want to do things right, your competition is out there taking your market by cutting corners. People are ready to short change customers in smart ways, bribe public officials, use substandard equipment and generally fail to deliver on promises. How do you compete with that? How is that a fair competition? Everyone going into business must understand this reality. You must accept it and then act appropriately to ensure your business is not forced out of the market. You should persevere and continue to educate people. You have to sell your values until you get more people to buy into your way of thinking.

Understanding that there is fierce competition is also why you might want to consider exploring niche markets rather than more general markets. Occupying a niche helps you to increase your chances of being noticed. In many industries or sectors, you will already have many players. What you want to do is to find that unique angle for your own business. It comes back to creating value. What is that thing you want to bring into the market? Speed? Safety? Comfort? Size? Height? Flexibility? Luxury? You can always find a niche to occupy. In the case of ABC Transport, it was comfort and safety that we introduced into an existing market. It defined us and gave us a uniqueness we were able to ride on for some years. The interesting thing about seeking out a niche market is that it takes you away from trying to beat the competition to creating your own unique space within the general market. Like Chan Kim and Renee Mauborgne said in their business classic, 'Blue Ocean Strategy':

'The only way to beat the competition, is to stop trying to beat the competition.'

They explained further,

"....instead of focusing on beating the competition, you focus on making the competition irrelevant by creating a leap in value for buyers and your company, thereby opening up new and uncontested market spaces...to fundamentally shift the strategy canvas of an industry, you must begin by reorienting your strategic focus from competitors to alternatives and from customers to noncustomers of the industry"

In a way, ABC Transport did this by creating a sub-industry within the existing road transport industry in Nigeria. We created an industry that was competing with the airlines – not the other road transport companies. Such did not exist before we got into the business. When you find a niche, you have found an untapped market space and the opportunity to make good profit. You have also found a way to expand the existing market boundaries. If you think like this, you will never be afraid of going into any market no matter how saturated it is because you can always carve out your own unique space. Industries never stand still. They evolve all the time and what makes them evolve are mostly the people who bring innovations and create niches within them.

3. People Function Best When Highly Valued

In the next chapter, I am going to focus on people but I can't resist the opportunity to chip this in here as one of those vital things I will mention to any curious young person in business.

I realized quickly that a business in which people are not valued, is one that will crumble. People make or mar any business. This sounds like something we all know but many people do not take it seriously enough. In our business, I noticed that a good driver can take a bad vehicle and manage it from Owerri to Lagos but a bad driver may fail to take a brand new vehicle from Owerri to Lagos.

A business is more about people that work to run it than we realize. A business is about its human resources. The successful business is the one where the founder can transmit his passion as much as possible to the outer layers of the organization. When a business starts, it is at times easy to be able to transmit the founder's spirit, vision, values and orientation to the first set of employees or managers. He can meet with them every day and they tend to understand what he wants and how he thinks.

But as the organization enlarges, other layers of the firm begin to develop and more people stop reporting directly to the founder. At that point, his ability to transmit his vision to all the layers will determine the organisation's success rate.

People are not numbers so don't treat them as such. They are critical to business success. Those who work with or for you have much more to give to you than you to them. If you can work well with people despite ethnic, religious or cultural differences, you will be a brilliant business leader.

People bring their backgrounds, beliefs, values, talents, dispositions and behaviour standards to work and these are the things that determine how they relate with others. They are potential trouble makers in any organisation. For your business to survive and grow well, you must understand these differences in people and be able to manage them well enough to the extent that they can be turned into advantages rather than problems. This is an aspect of leadership in business that one can learn. At ABC, we have always had a very diverse set of workers. Because Nigeria has hundreds of ethnic groups, it is easy to understand why managing ethnic and religious differences can be tricky for organisations in the country. But when you create an environment where values, standards and performance quality are the focus, people, despite their differences, can unite to achieve success for your organisation.

It has been an advantage to me as an entrepreneur and business leader, to be someone who pays little attention to the tribes and religion of those who work with me while focusing almost entirely on the values they bring to the work table.

4. Money Is Overrated

I am convinced that the importance of money in business is over rated. Ideas trump money every single time in business. Money follows ideas. Ideas determine where money is spent or invested. If we were to use human analogy, idea is the mother and money is the offspring. If you have money but lack the right ideas, you will lose that money. People say, "If I see two million naira now I will start a business," But when you ask them, "What kind of business will you start? ", they respond, "I don't know. I will think about it". Someone else who understands how it works will say, "I have this idea and I am looking for money to execute it. Would you like to look at my plan? It might interest you."

So, while some seek money, the wise ones seek ideas that can provide services and products for people. It is important to understand this and it is the reason why you see many people retire, get paid huge sums of money yet get broke within two to three years after retirement. If you check them out you will discover they were never ready for life after retirement. They never explored ideas and planned on how to execute them. When money came, they simply wasted it because they lacked ideas.

Don't get me wrong, money is very important in business and I am not insinuating that it isn't. If you go into business thinking money is unimportant or you don't understand its dynamics, you will end up frustrated. At the very core of business is profit making. A business that consistently fails to make money, will fold up. The entrepreneur must have an eye for making money. That knack for identifying the product or service that will sell well, is an essential trait of the business entrepreneur. Without it, you might as well be running a not-for profit organisation.

So, make no mistake about it, you must go into business to make money. But my point is that money is a product, a result, a consequence of focusing primarily on creating value. It should not be an end but a means to an end. You cannot start out with the mind-set of wanting nothing but to make profit at any cost. You cannot succeed if, when you deal with customers, all you are thinking about is how to earn money from them. You cannot put money before ideas. You cannot spend all your time as a start-up, searching for money to run a business you have not thought through in terms of the type of products and services it will provide and the way you should best provide those services.

For the intending start-up, money must be set aside for a while to work through the core idea of the business. Do you want to offer speed or quantity? Do you want to create a process that will make your product cheaper for customers hence save them money? Do you want to make access to your service easier than others for your customers? Do you want to offer more options or varieties? Do you want to offer a different look and feel, thus offer customers more class and appeal to their status? Do you want to take a local product to the national or international stages? Do you want to entertain better? Do you want to make people feel safer? You have to sort the idea out first and plan how you will execute it before you start thinking about money. Too many people flip this and have wrong priorities as they prepare to get into business. It is the same with those who are already into business. Ideas, values and people must always be seen to be more important than money. The moment a business misses this, all sorts of problems will follow.

5. You Can't Succeed Without Help or Favours

Again this is related to people but it is worth highlighting here. It is important for someone starting out in business to understand that things do not always go according to plan and that one needs support to get ahead at times. While I say this, I do not think it is smart to wait on God or providence or men to get things done. Even though I believe that God ultimately blesses us, I am not someone who will not prepare for an opportunity because I want to go to Church to pray for help. I believe opportunity often meets preparation. If you prepare yourself, opportunity will come your way. When you are prepared for something and an opportunity comes for it, you will profit from the situation.

Nevertheless, everyone needs a leverage and people give us leverages in life. As a young entrepreneur, if you are diligent, hardworking, visionary and generally appear to be on top of your game, you will get help often. Someone once gave me his property and said, "Give it to the bank as collateral. I will sign it off." He must have seen something in me that encouraged him to take such a risk. Unfortunately, the man is no longer alive but I'm still close to his family. More experienced and successful entrepreneurs have an eye for young entrepreneurs with potential and they are often willing to back them up in different ways. I have met young people I believed in and supported. I have given out money to young people with ideas because they looked like they knew what they were doing and were clear about what they wanted to accomplish. I don't just throw money around or waste time, so I am careful in such situations. But it is not too difficult to see through young entrepreneurs who have it in them to succeed.

It is extremely tough to succeed in business without favours. The person who understands this and constantly builds a good reputation and positions himself to receive such support, is wise. Positioning yourself means having integrity, being trustworthy, having good character and generally oozing out competence.

Prayer alone won't make things happen for you. In Nigeria, we tend to rely too much on prayer while we fail to do the things we are supposed to do to make things work. This is not smart, and it will only make us mediocre and fail in achieving things. Prepare, study, do all the necessary work and position yourself through your actions, to receive favours.

In our company, we have more than 1,500 employees. I run a very open system, everybody knows what I earn and they know when the company has money and when we don't have enough cash. Nothing is hidden so if salaries are delayed, nobody will say, "The MD is enjoying while we are suffering". What they have done is to set up a corporative society. Each staff saves money in this cooperative and at a point in time they had so much money that they even offered to help when we hit a cash crunch period. Some of them came to me and said, "Oga, we know the company is struggling. Can't we give you money from the cooperative to buy buses? We know the bank interest rates are high so getting money from the cooperative will be cheaper for you. Just tell us how much interest rate you can afford." That is trust. When we were going public, almost every staff remained at the company because they believed in what we were doing. They didn't see it as Frank's family business because we positioned ourselves to receive that kind of favour from them. A few years ago when things got difficult, I called the staff and said, "It is either we retrench, or we take salary cuts". They went ahead to take salary cuts. That's favour right there and our staff could only grant it because we did things right and earned their trust over time.

Usually it is character that attracts favours and like I have said, progress becomes very limited, if not impossible, without favours. This is why when people talk about being self-made, I tend to disagree with the notion. I don't think anyone is self-made because we all need a support system. We need people to work with us. We can't do it alone. Are you self-made when you have an idea but need people to help you execute it? No, you are not. I am usually given the credit for where ABC Transport is today being the founder but there are other people who suffered to make things work. So, being self-made in absolute terms, is contradictory to the process that makes anyone successful.

Ideas are more important
than money in business.

Unless you create value for
people, you can't make money.

To build a successful business,
you need a vision.

No one is self-made,
we all need help.

A business that does not
make profits consistently,
will fold up.

Creating value for people is
what attracts money.

CHAPTER TWELVE

People Determine Everything
"You will fail in business if you don't understand people"

In the previous chapter, I wrote about the importance of people in business. Nevertheless, for the purpose of emphasis and to point out a few significant things I did not mention, I decided the subject is worth a chapter on its own. Understanding people and human nature is key in business. Things like learning how to carry people along, helping them understand their roles and how best to successfully function there and motivating employees with rewards for good performance are important skills to apply in business. It becomes easier if you are empathetic rather than merely manipulating people to do things for you.

I have often asked: "If ABC Transport is successful, are my people proud to be part of it? Have I been able to convince them that they made the success happen or do I tend to ascribe all the praise to myself? Do I challenge them enough? Do they participate in the decision-making processes?"

Let's say I want to start a new route to Lokoja and I've worked out what it is going to take - the pros and cons. When I call for a meeting, rather than give instructions on moving to Lokoja, I prefer to get everyone talking about the possibility. If I am absolutely convinced it is the right decision to make, I prefer to guide the conversation in such a way that everybody agrees that Lokoja is a good idea. By doing it that way, the decision can be accepted as a collective, rather than a dictatorial one. As a leader you usually have your preferences but you don't need to always order people around. You can engage them. You can guide them to see why your choice will benefit everybody. You can make them part of the whole process. Getting people's buy-in encourages them to join hands with you to achieve success and the key is to make sure the business is about everybody involved and not just you. Your staff are not going to be confident in the system if they don't see anything beyond you and your family. You need to institutionalize the business to give everyone a sense of being involved in something bigger than any individual.

At ABC Transport, we have a Board of Directors that is the ultimate decision-making body. We have managers, committees, systems and structures that make the organisation run daily. Everybody knows that Frank Nneji is just one man in the entire system even though he is the founder and MD. The system runs itself. People see this and it gives them the assurance that they are part of a big organisation.

Trust Your People and They Will Trust You

I understood early that not only must you give people a sense of being involved in something big and important, you must also deeply trust them. I know this is a tricky one because human nature can disappoint but not much can be achieved if those who work for or with you don't have a sense of being trusted by you.

You must believe that people can do things right on their own. People come to me and say, "The problem with transport business is that the drivers are useless. You cannot manage them. They are all rogues."

"No, my drivers are not like that," I usually respond, "ABC drivers are different." I tell them this because I truly believe it. It doesn't mean we don't have bad drivers, we do. But we must give them benefit of the doubt. I say things like, "We trust you. We know you can do it. You are good people. My drivers are the best drivers you can find".

When you tell a man that, he becomes expectant. He strives to be exactly that. People say, "No matter what you give them, they steal." What those that say that don't realize is that if you believe someone will steal from you and you keep saying it, the person might just steal from you one day.

If you say, "I don't trust anybody," while your employees are there with you, how do you want them to trust you? Everything we've done at ABC has been about people. The buses and the trucks don't run on their own. People run them and for them to do so, you need to show that you trust them.

But I understand people who are very sceptical about this line of thought. You can easily get burnt when you trust people too much. There are bad eggs in every organisation and one must be realistic about that. But that doesn't mean we should condemn everybody.

Pay Attention to Everything, Even the Job Labels

In our industry, the law makes it mandatory that if you carry a particular number of people in a bus, you must have a conductor. At ABC, our conductors are called attendants. That change in name did great magic. It made our attendants feel a sense of dignity and sophistication. The way drivers and attendants dress also matters. Ours dress in nice uniforms that make them look very professional. This is why some of our attendants are law graduates. We have made the job look decent to the extent that graduates are happy to take it up with a sense of pride. So, as a business leader or entrepreneur, you don't allow anything or anyone to make your staff feel inferior. A lot of that has to do with how you label their jobs and treat them. When we want to hire, we tell them, "We are not taking you as conductors. If you come as conductors, you're just going to conduct the bus which is inanimate. What we want you to do is to attend to people, serve them and support the driver". That immediately influences how they see themselves and their job.

Be Simple

One thing that also helps to build trust is when you are simple. I have personally experienced this. Although with the type of system we run, people don't need me to solve basic problems, nevertheless, anyone, including the drivers, can easily reach me if the situation demands for it. I get text messages from drivers regularly.

I could make myself inaccessible but how will that benefit the organisation? Being easy to reach and approach, builds trust. When people get through to me within the organisation, I try to attend to their issues as quickly as possible. This also helps one to get feedback. Once you are easily reachable or approachable, people tend to trust you more and once that trust is there, they give you useful feedback.

Be Principled

Initially people found me difficult to deal with because I didn't fit into the stereotypes they had in mind. There were all sorts of theories about me. Some said I was tight fisted and that I was never happy to give or share money. But they just didn't understand me. I was trying to build a business, a strong brand. It meant that I had to make tough choices and stay focused on what I was trying to do. Family members expected that they would ask and I would give them jobs within the organisation but that didn't happen. I believe people should earn jobs based on merit. I had to draw a line between personal relationships and business. Of course, this earned me criticism. A lot of family members come to write our job tests. We take those that pass and reject those that fail. It is as simple as that, no sentiments attached. It's easier to get them in for industrial attachment or National Youth Service roles but when it comes to full time jobs, it's a totally different ball game. I had this cousin who did her youth service with us. She took what we called 'Transport Officer (I) Test' (TO1 Test) and flopped. Then her father came to solicit for her. He asked, "What do you want her to do?" I responded, "She didn't pass the examination, so we can't hire her. But we can give her a chance to take the test again." I turned to her and asked, "Are you ready to take the test again?" she said she couldn't be ready until another two days. "Okay, come back in two days to re-do the test", I said. She returned in two days, sat for the test and failed it again. There was nothing I could do at that point. I was not going to force her into the system because she was my cousin.

In Nigeria, people in business deal with this type of challenge all the time. Family members and kinsmen put you under pressure to hire based on sentiments. One must never yield to such. An advantage of being related to me is that you will probably know when there is a vacancy to be filled. When I go to the village to see my mother, people come to me with CVs. I collect them and give them a fair chance of being hired. But that's where it stops. If they fail our recruitment processes, then they don't get the job. If they pass, they get hired. It is as straightforward as that. Fortunately, our staff at ABC Transport have come to understand this side of me and in a way, it is part of what keeps me simple. I guess it makes me easy to read and easy to predict. I mentioned earlier that when we first started ABC Transport, some drivers were not happy that we were taking off without the buses being filled. They wanted me to allow them to pick up passengers along the way but I refused. I insisted on keeping to our plan and outlined standards. It was a good thing that I didn't change my stance because it eventually paid off.

Sticking to standards was not something we did because we were a Plc. It was something that helped us become a Plc. If you run through our organisation, you will find clear processes that dictate everything. For instance, everybody knows I can't just fire someone. If I fire you and you feel unfairly treated, you can appeal to the human resources management committee which consists of members of staff who will review your case fairly, based on company policies. I remember when KPMG visited ABC Transport to do due diligence ahead of Capital Alliance's equity investment into our company. They were amazed that a private company could practice corporate governance that much. Capital Alliance eventually bought 30% shares in ABC Transport in 2003.

The point is that people respond to how they are treated and you had better not doubt for once that they are watching and assessing you. If you understand this about people, then you have a big advantage when it comes to running a business.

People want to be recognized.

People want to be appreciated.

People want to be rewarded.

People want to grow.

People want to be trusted.

People want opportunities.

People want to be treated fairly.

Index